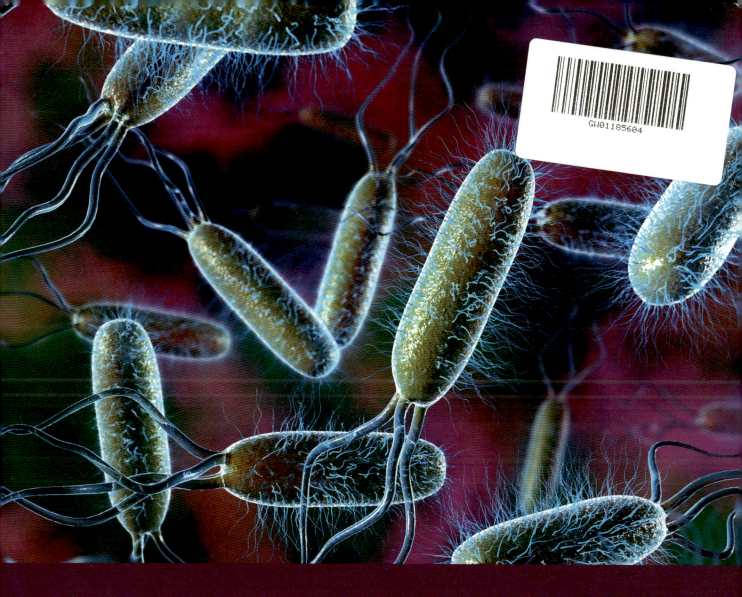

THE GOOD, THE BAD & THE UGLY

MICROBES

DARIEL BURDASS

    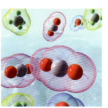

The Good, The Bad & The Ugly – Microbes

The Good, The Bad & The Ugly – Microbes, a resource for secondary schools, explores how microbes can be both friend and foe and most importantly, why we all need these invisible organisms to live. A CD-ROM accompanies this book which provides a comprhensive, full colour PowerPoint™ presentation on each of the 5 topics covered in the book. The CD-ROM also provides extension material and a range of student activities.

Author: Dariel Burdass
Editor: Janet Hurst
Designer and Production Editor: Dariel Burdass
Proofreader: Yvonne Taylor

Acknowledgements
Thanks are due to Professor Jo Verran (Manchester Metropolitan University) and Dr Colin Bielby (Manchester Metropolitan University) for their helpful comments on the text. Every care has been taken to ensure that the information provided in *The Good, The Bad & The Ugly – Microbes* is correct, but the author will be pleased to learn of any errors that have remained undetected.

Published by The Society for General Microbiology (SGM)
Marlborough House
Basingstoke Road
Spencers Wood
RG7 1AG, UK

First published 2009
ISBN: 978-0-9536838-5-7
© SGM 2009

CONTENTS

Introducing microbes

What are microbes?	2
Introducing microbes	2
Classification – How organisms are grouped together	4
The microbial groups	7
How microbes move	13
How did life begin?	14

Microbes and the human body

Microbes and disease	16
Invading microbes	16
How do microbes make us feel ill?	21
How are microbes spread?	22
How can we stop the spread of diseases?	24
Preventing disease through vaccination	25
Treating disease	27
Microbes and sexually transmitted infections	31

Microbes and food

Microbes and food production	36
Food from fungi	36
Food spoilage	38
Food preservation	39
Food poisoning	40

Microbes and the outdoors

The role of microbes in recycling	42
Getting rid of rubbish	46
Sewage treatment	47
Cleaning up with microbes	48
Is it a fungus? Is it an alga? No, it's lichen!	49

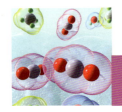

Microbes and climate change

What is climate change?	52
Can microbes help save the planet?	53
How are microbes contributing to global warming?	54
Microbes and biofuels	56
The impact of climate change on health	59
Glossary	60
Index	64
Picture credits	66

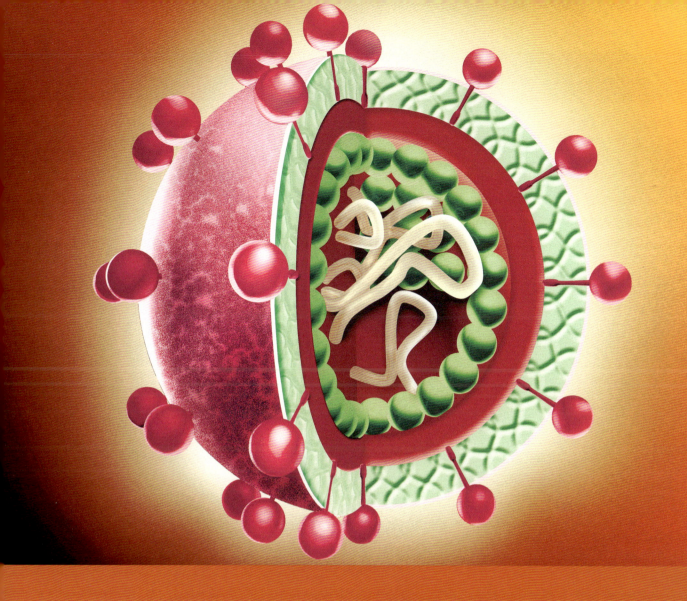

INTRODUCING MICROBES

CHAPTER 1

INTRODUCING MICROBES

What are microbes?

Micro-organisms can be friend or foe but most importantly, we all need them to live!

> **Definition**
>
> Micro = small
>
> Organism = living creature

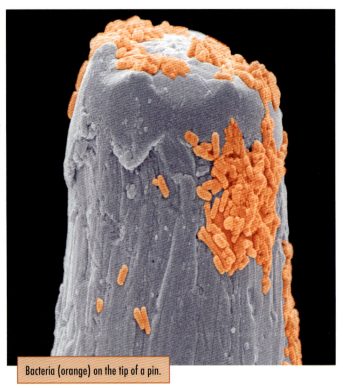
Bacteria (orange) on the tip of a pin.

Introducing microbes

Micro-organisms, or microbes for short, are very small living organisms, so small that most of them are invisible. The majority can only be seen with a microscope, which magnifies their image to make them look much larger. In fact microbes are so tiny you would find over a million in a teaspoon of soil. They make up more than 60 % of the Earth's living matter and scientists estimate that 2-3 billion species share the planet with us.

> The diagram below highlights the sizes of different microbes and compares them to other living things

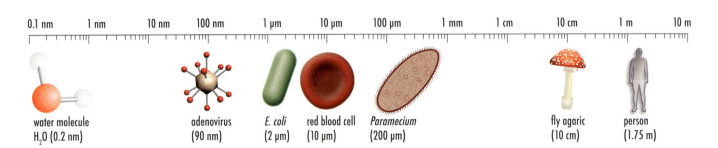

Microbes, like all living things, are made up of cells. Cells are the building blocks of life. They are the smallest structural unit in an organism which can function independently; many of them are specialized for particular jobs. Cells can function together as part of a tissue such as muscle, or an organ like the heart in animals, or independently as free-living organisms like an *Amoeba*, which is a single celled microbe.

INTRODUCING MICROBES 3

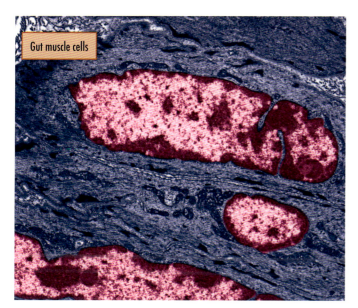
Gut muscle cells

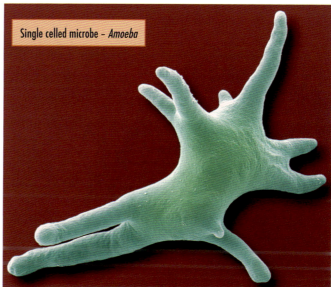
Single celled microbe - *Amoeba*

History
Louis Pasteur

In the 1860s Louis Pasteur (1822-1895), a French scientist, performed an experiment that finally disproved the theory of spontaneous generation.

From the time of the ancient Romans until the late 19th century, most people believed that simple life forms such as microbes and small creatures like worms could come to life spontaneously from non-living matter. They believed that spontaneous generation mainly occurred in decaying material such as food that had been left out and had gone rotten. Pasteur had already shown that there were many microbial cells in the air and that these microbes were similar to the ones found in decaying substances. He thought that the microbes in the decaying matter came from the air and not by spontaneous generation and set out to prove his theory. He predicated that a container of sterile, germ-free beef soup would remain sterile, even if exposed to the air, as long as microbes were prevented from entering the flask. He used special 'swan necked' flasks with long S-shaped stems for the experiment. These were designed to let air in but trapped the dust and air-borne microbes in the neck of the flask, preventing it from reaching the sterile contents. Over time he observed the flasks. He found that the soup in the flasks remained sterile and did not decay. However if he tilted the flask so that it was at an angle, the dust and microbes could enter and the soup soon swarmed with microbial life. This proved Pasteur's theory and disproved spontaneous generation.

Pasteur also invented the process of pasteurization that helps to preserve food and drink, discovered 'the germ theory of disease' which proved that microbes are the cause of infectious diseases, and developed vaccines for several infectious diseases, including rabies.

Micro-organisms occur in an amazing variety of shapes and sizes and they are divided into one of 6 groups which are explained in more detail later on.

Fungi	page 7	Algae	page 10
Bacteria	page 11	Protozoa	page 11
Archaea	page 13	Viruses	page 13

Classification - How organisms are grouped together

We are surrounded by vast quantities of living things, ranging from the largest tree down to the smallest microbe. Due to the enormous variety of organisms that exist, scientists have arranged all living things into groups. This is called classification or taxonomy. At first organisms were distinguished from one another by characteristics that could be seen with the naked eye. Later on organisms were examined in more detail using first optical microscopes and then more powerful electron microscopes. Today most scientists use a system which is based on an organism's genetic make up to decide which group it belongs to.

Changes in classification over time

Linnaeus 1730s 2 Kingdoms	Haeckel 1866 3 Kingdoms	Chatton 1937 2 Domains	Copeland 1938/1947 4 Kingdoms	Whittaker 1968 5 Kingdoms	Woese et al. 1990 3 Domains
	Protista	Prokaryotes	Monera	Monera	Bacteria
					Archaea
			Protoctista	Protoctista	
Vegetabilia	Plantae	Eukaryotes	Plantae	Fungi	Eukarya
				Plantae	
Animalia	Animalia		Animalia	Animalia	

Classification began in the 1730s when Carl Linnaeus, who is known as the father of taxonomy, divided all living things into two Kingdoms.

| Animalia Kingdom contained all organisms that ate, moved and grew to a certain size then stopped

| Vegetabilia Kingdom contained all organisms that didn't move or eat and continued to grow throughout their lives

When protozoa, algae and bacteria were discovered Linnaeus put the motile protozoa into the Animalia Kingdom and the algae and bacteria into the Vegetabilia Kingdom because they appeared to be static. The Vegetabilia Kingdom was renamed Plantae Kingdom.

In 1866 another scientist called Ernst Haeckel introduced a third Kingdom called the Protista. At this point fungi were also regarded as plants and were included in the Plantae Kingdom. The remaining single-celled organisms, which included algae, bacteria and protozoa, were put into the Protista Kingdom. During this period multicellular seaweeds were thought to resemble plants, not algae, and were included in the Plantae Kingdom.

Carl Linnaeus

INTRODUCING MICROBES

Hot springs at Yellow Stone Park, USA

A French microbiologist called Edouard Chatton was studying the cellular structure of organisms in the Protista Kingdom. He found that there were two distinctly different groups based on their cellular organisation. He called these two groups

| Prokaryotes

| Eukaryotes

The algae and protozoa were put into the group Eukaryotes because they had a membrane bound nucleus (see page 6). The bacteria were put in the group Prokaryotes because they lacked a membrane bound nucleus. In 1937 Chatton reported that plants and animals were also Eukaryotes.

In 1938 the botanist Herbert Copeland introduced an additional Kingdom for bacteria and named it Monera. The Protista Kingdom now only contained unicellular eukaryotes, and in 1947, in order to stress this difference from the 'old' Protists, he used the term Protoctista instead.

Opinions between scientists, as is often the case, differed and not everybody used this 4 Kingdom classification system. The ecologist Robert Whittaker recognised that fungi were very different from plants, and needed their own Kingdom. This resulted in the 5 Kingdom classification system, which was proposed in 1968 and is still the standard system taught in schools today.

| Prokaryotes — the Kingdom Monera which contains the bacteria

| Eukaryotes — the other four Kingdoms, Fungi, Protoctista, Plantae and Animalia

It was also decided that seaweeds were closer to single-celled algae than green plants and they were moved from the Plantae to the Protoctista Kingdom. This meant that this kingdom now contained multi-cellular as well as single-celled organisms.

During the 1970s a completely new group of organisms was discovered in the boiling hot springs in Yellow Stone Park, USA by Carl Woese and his colleagues at the University of Illinois. As these organisms had no nucleus and, under a microscope, resembled bacteria they were called archaebacteria. Following genetic research which analysed the RNA of the archaebacteria Woese argued that they were so different from bacteria they needed their own group. In 1990 he and his colleagues came up with the 3 Domain classification system which divided living things into three groups based on their genetic similarity: it is used by most scientists today. This system assumes that there was a universal ancestor cell that gave rise to three different cell types, each representing a domain. The three Domains are

- Bacteria
- Archaea
- Eukarya.

Viruses are not usually included in any system as they are non-cellular and are dependent on a host cell for their replication and metabolic processes. (see page 13)

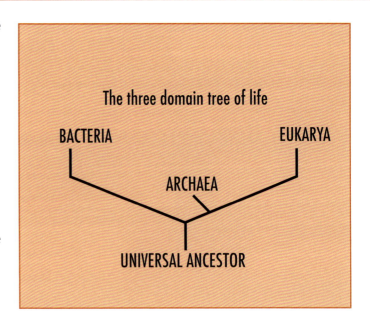

Factlet
What is a nucleus?

A nucleus is a membrane-bound structure. It is the control centre of a cell and is also where all the genetic information, the DNA, is found. The DNA is in long continuous pieces called chromosomes. Each chromosome is divided into basic units called genes. Genes contain all the biological information needed to build and maintain a living example of a particular organism. This includes all the data that allow the organism to function as well as the instructions that determine the organism's appearance, health and behaviour. The complete set of genes in an organism is known as its genome. Usually the more complex an organism, the bigger its genome.

In prokaryotes the genetic information is contained in a single loop of DNA and not in a membrane-bound structure. As a result prokaryotes have no nucleus. Some bacteria have an extra circle of genetic material, called a plasmid. The plasmid often contains genes that give the bacterium some advantage over other bacteria. For example it may have a gene that makes the bacterium resistant to a certain antibiotic (see page 27). This is an advantage for the bacterium because antibiotics kill bacteria or stop them from growing. So if the bacterium is resistant to a certain antibiotic then it can't be harmed or destroyed by it.

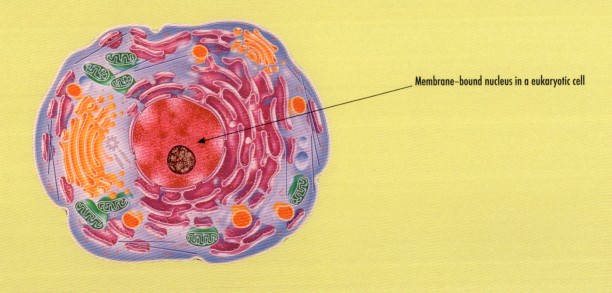

Membrane-bound nucleus in a eukaryotic cell

INTRODUCING MICROBES

Factlet
Extremophiles

Sometimes archaea are referred to as extremophiles because the first ones were discovered growing in harsh habitats such as hot springs. This name is not part of the classification system and it can be confusing to use because not all archaea live in extreme environments. Extremophile is a term used to describe any microbe living in an environment where life would not normally be expected to exist.

Thermophiles grow best at temperatures of 50 – 70 °C. Some, hyperthermophiles, need it even hotter and they grow best at 100 °C and above (that's the temperature at which water boils)! On land they live in compost heaps, landfills, boiling hot springs and geysers such as those found in Yellow Stone Park, USA.

Microbes called psychrophiles grow best at lower temperatures between -10 – 20 °C. They can even survive in ice. They are mainly found in the Arctic and Antarctic oceans which remain frozen for most of the year. Psychrophiles are often responsible for spoilage in refrigerated foods, particularly dairy products such as milk. Very little is known about them. Scientists are trying to find out if these cold loving microbes could live in the frozen wastes of planet Mars.

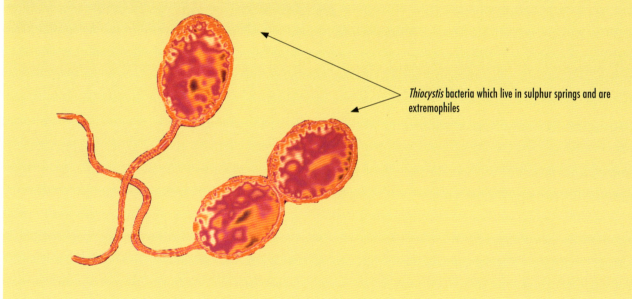

Thiocystis bacteria which live in sulphur springs and are extremophiles

The microbial groups

Fungi

Fungi can be single celled or very complex multicellular organisms. They are found in just about any habitat but most live on the land, mainly in soil or on plant material rather than in sea or fresh water. A group called the decomposers grow in the soil or on dead plant matter where they play an important role in the recycling of carbon and other elements (see page 42). Some are parasites of plants causing diseases such as mildews, rusts, scabs or canker. In crops fungal diseases can lead to significant monetary loss for the farmer. A very small number of fungi cause diseases in animals. In humans these include skin diseases such as athletes' foot and thrush.

Types of fungi

Fungi are subdivided further on the basis of their life cycles, the presence or structure of their fruiting body and the arrangement of and type of spores (reproductive or distributional cells) they produce. The three major groups of fungi are:

> multicellular filamentous moulds
>
> macroscopic filamentous fungi that form large fruiting bodies. Sometimes the group is referred to as 'mushrooms', but the mushroom is just the part of the fungus we see above ground which is also known as the fruiting body.
>
> single celled microscopic yeasts

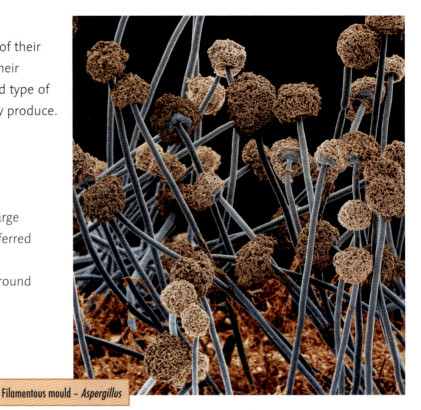

Filamentous mould - *Aspergillus*

Multicellular filamentous moulds

Moulds are made up of very fine threads (hyphae). Hyphae grow at the tip and divide repeatedly along their length creating long and branching chains. (See diagram page 9.) Hyphae are very strong which enables them to penetrate tough woody plant cell walls and the hard skeletons that form the outside of insects' bodies. The hyphae keep branching and growing and intertwining until they form a network. This network of threads, called a mycelium, is usually hidden under the bark of rotten trees or in the soil under mounds of leaf litter (rotting leaves). It can easily be seen without a microscope. Special chemicals called enzymes are secreted from the hyphal tip. These enzymes break down the organic matter found in the soil into smaller molecules which are soluble and can be absorbed through the hyphal wall and used by the fungus as food. Some of the hyphal branches grow into the air and on these aerial branches spores are formed. Spores are specialized structures with a protective coat that shields them from harsh environmental conditions such as drying out and high temperatures. They are so small that between 500 – 1000 could fit on a pin head.

Spores are similar to seeds as they enable the fungus to reproduce. Spores are spread by wind, rain, or insects. They eventually land in new habitats and if conditions are right, they start to grow and produce new hyphae (see page 9). As fungi can't move they use spores to find a new environment with fewer competing organisms. Examples of moulds include *Penicillium* and *Rhizopus*.

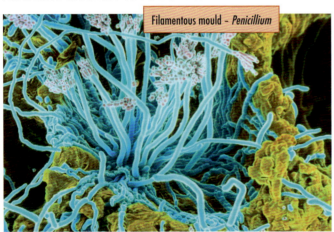

Filamentous mould - *Penicillium*

Filamentous mould - *Rhizopus*

INTRODUCING MICROBES

How a mycelium is formed and how spores are distributed

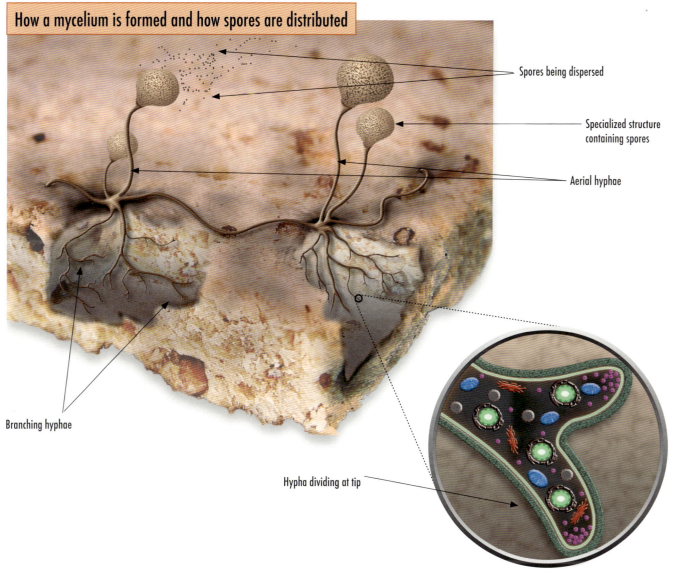

- Spores being dispersed
- Specialized structure containing spores
- Aerial hyphae
- Branching hyphae
- Hypha dividing at tip

Filamentous fungus *Amanita*

Macroscopic filamentous fungi

Macroscopic filamentous fungi also grow by producing a mycelium below ground. They differ from moulds because they produce visible fruiting bodies (commonly known as mushrooms or toadstools) that hold the spores. The fruiting body is made up of tightly packed hyphae which divide to produce the different parts of the fungal structure, for example the cap and the stem. Gills underneath the cap are covered with spores and a 10 cm diameter cap can produce up to 100 million spores per hour. Examples of macroscopic filamentous fungi are *Morchella* (morels), *Rigidoporus* (bracket fungus) and *Amanita* (fly agaric mushroom).

INTRODUCING MICROBES

Yeasts

Yeasts are small, lemon-shaped single cells that are about the same size as red blood cells. They multiply by budding a daughter cell off from the original parent cell. The bud continues to grow until it is approximately the same size as the original cell. Then the nucleus divides, so that each cell has a nucleus, and the two cells separate. Scars can be seen on the surface of the yeast cell where buds have broken off. Each yeast cell can usually undergo the budding process between 12 and 15 times, after which it is no longer capable of dividing and multiplying. Yeasts play an important role in the production of bread and in brewing (see page 37). Yeasts are also one of the most widely used model organisms for genetic studies, for example in cancer research. Other species of yeast are opportunistic pathogens and cause infections in individuals who do not have a healthy immune system. This can sometimes be due to recurrent infections, chemotherapy or antibiotics. Well known yeasts are *Saccharomyces,* used in brewing, and *Candida* a potential human pathogen.

Budding yeast cells. Scars can be seen on the surface

Factlet
Giant fungus
The largest organism in the world, when measured by area, is the Honey Mushroom fungus, *Armillaria ostoyae*! Its tangled mat of hyphae covers a gigantic 8.9 km² in Malheur National Forest in The Blue Mountains of eastern Oregon, USA. All that can be seen above the ground are the mushrooms that erupt from the soil at the base of infected trees.

Algae

Algae can exist as single cells, an example of which is *Chlamydomonas*, or joined together in chains like *Spirogyra* or made up of many cells, for instance *Rhodymenia* (red seaweed).

Most algae live in fresh or sea water where they can either be free-floating (planktonic) or attached to the bottom. Some algae can grow on rocks, soil or vegetation as long as there is enough moisture. A few algae form very close partnerships with fungi to form lichens (see page 49). Unusual algal habitats are the hairs of the South American Sloth and Polar bears.

All algae contain a pigment called chlorophyll *a* (other types of chlorophyll such as *b*, *c* and *l* or *d* may also be present) and they make their own food by photosynthesis (see page 42). The chlorophyll is contained in the chloroplasts and gives many algae their green appearance. However some algae appear brown, yellow or red because in addition to chlorophylls they have other accessory pigments that camouflage the green colour. These accessory pigments may be used to perform photosynthesis.

INTRODUCING MICROBES

Spirogyra

Rhodymenia

Protozoa

Protozoa are single celled organisms. They come in many different shapes and sizes ranging from an *Amoeba* (see page 3) which can change its shape to *Paramecium* with its fixed shape and complex structure. They live in a wide variety of moist habitats including fresh water, marine environments and the soil. Some are parasitic, which means they live in other plants and animals including humans, where they cause disease. *Plasmodium,* for example, causes malaria.

Paramecium

Bacteria

Bacteria are single celled microbes. They are classified into 5 groups according to their basic shapes: spherical (cocci), rod (bacilli), spiral (spirilla), comma (vibrios) or corkscrew (spirochaetes). They can exist as single cells, in pairs, chains or clusters.

The different bacterial shapes

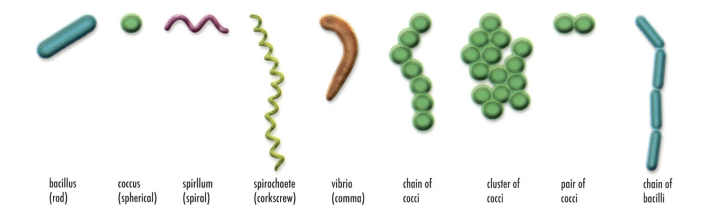

bacillus (rod) | coccus (spherical) | spirllum (spiral) | spirochaete (corkscrew) | vibrio (comma) | chain of cocci | cluster of cocci | pair of cocci | chain of bacilli

Bacteria are found living in every habitat on Earth including on and in humans. There are approximately 10 times as many bacterial cells as human cells in the human body. A lot of those bacterial cells are found lining the digestive system (see page 18).

A typical bacterial cell

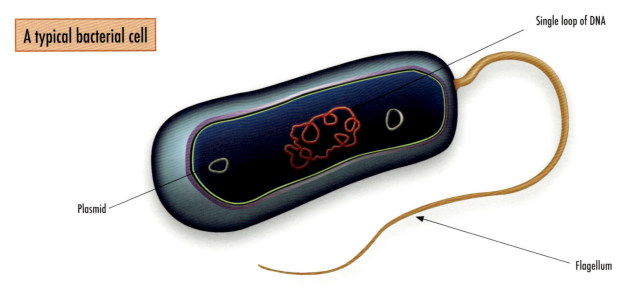

Single loop of DNA
Plasmid
Flagellum

Factlet
How do bacteria reproduce?
Bacteria reproduce by binary fission. In this process the bacterium, which is a single cell, divides into two identical daughter cells. Binary fission begins when the DNA of the bacterium divides into two (replicates). The bacterial cell then elongates and splits into two daughter cells each with identical DNA to the parent cell. Each daughter cell is a clone of the parent cell.

When conditions are favourable such as the right temperature and nutrients are available, some bacteria such as *Escherichia coli* can divide every 20 minutes. This means that in just 7 hours one bacterium can generate 2,097,152 bacteria. After one more hour the number of bacteria will have risen to a colossal 16,777,216. That's why we can quickly become ill when pathogenic microbes invade our bodies.

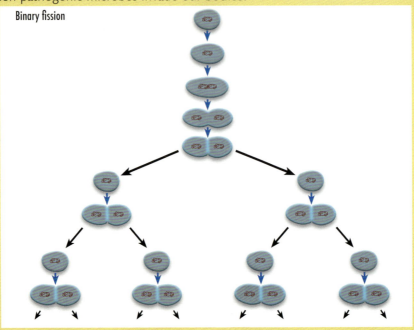

Binary fission

INTRODUCING MICROBES

Archaea

Archaea were among the first forms of life that emerged on Earth billions of years ago. Originally scientists only isolated archaea from harsh environments. However many archaeans have now been discovered living in ordinary environments; some even live in human guts! Methanogens are archaea that convert carbon dioxide to methane in a process called methanogenesis (see page 54).

Archaea can be spherical, rod, spiral, lobed, rectangular or irregular in shape. An unusual flat square-shaped species that lives in salty pools has also been discovered. Some exist as single cells, others form filaments or clusters.

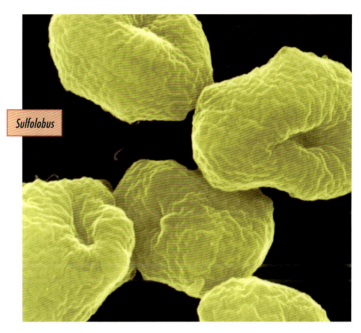

Sulfolobus

Viruses

Viruses are the smallest of all the microbes. They are said to be so small that 500 million rhinoviruses (which cause the common cold) could fit on to the head of a pin. They are unique because they are only alive and able to multiply inside the cells of other living things. The cell they multiply in is called the host cell.

A virus is made up of a core of genetic material, either DNA or RNA, surrounded by a protective coat called a capsid which is made up of protein. Sometimes the capsid is surrounded by an additional spikey coat called the envelope. Viruses are capable of latching onto host cells and getting inside them.

Viruses only exist to make more viruses. The virus particle attaches to the host cell before penetrating it. The virus then uses the host cell's machinery to replicate its own genetic material. Once replication has been completed the virus particles leave the host by either budding or bursting out of the cell (lysis).

Budding

As the newly formed viral particle pushes against the host cell's plasma membrane a portion adheres to it. The plasma membrane envelops the virus becoming the viral envelope. The virus is released from the cell. This process slowly uses up the host's cell membrane and usually leads to cell death.

Lysis

The virus particles burst out of the host cell into the extracellular space resulting in the death of the host cell.

Once the virus has escaped from the host cell it is ready to enter a new cell and multiply.

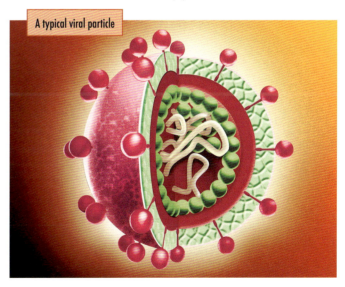

A typical viral particle

How microbes move

Motility in microbes is very important as it allows them to move away from harmful environments and towards more advantageous surroundings. The stimulus for movement can either be chemicals, light or oxygen.

INTRODUCING MICROBES

Movement in microbes is either by:-

Cilia
Cilia are tiny-hair like structures that cover the outside of a microbe making it look hairy. They beat in a regular continuous pattern like flexible oars.

Flagella
Flagella are long thread-like structures that extend from the cell surface. They can be situated at one or both ends of the microbe either singly or in groups that resemble tufts, or they can be found in many places dotted around the surface of the microbe. In eukaryotes the flagellum moves in a whip-like motion that produces waves that propel the microbe around. In prokaryotes the flagellum produces movement by rotating like a corkscrew.

Cellular deformation or amoeboid movement
This type of movement can only occur in microbes without a rigid cell wall. The organism moves by sending out pseudopodia, temporary protrusions that fill with cytoplasm that flows from the body of the cell. Pseudopodia can occur at any point on the cell surface and can vary in number. They attach to the adjacent surface, such as soil particles, and then pull the rest of the cell towards the pseudopodia.

Gliding motility
The microbe glides slowly over a solid surface.

Microbial motility

	CILIA	FLAGELLA	AMOEBOID	GLIDING
PROKARYOTES	✗	✓	✗	✓
FUNGI	✗	✗	✗	✗
ALGAE	✗	✓	✗	✓
PROTOZOA	✓	✓	✓	✗

Viruses are a special case. Inside our bodies they attach to and then hitch rides on cells in blood and lymph until they reach the cell they want to infect. Outside, they are carried in the water droplets we sneeze out, and on air currents, water, food, faeces, vomit or other animals.

How did life begin?

Microbes have been around for at least 3,500 million years and were the only life forms on Earth for most of that time. As the Earth cooled, liquid water formed and the first microbial life appeared. The conditions on Earth in the beginning were very hostile so the first microbes probably resembled the Archaea, as they were able to live in the extreme environments such as the high temperature found on the cooling planet.

Around 2,800 million years ago, cyanobacteria, the largest and most diverse group of photosynthetic bacteria, probably appeared. This was an important development as these were the first organisms able to carry out aerobic photosynthesis (see page 42). It is thought that cyanobacteria were responsible for raising the level of oxygen in the Earth's atmosphere from less than 1 % to the 21 % of today. The presence of oxygen in the atmosphere allowed the evolution of new aerobic (oxygen using) species of microbes, which began to colonize every habitat on the planet.

Different species of cyanobacteria formed complex microbial communities, with other types of microbes as they evolved, and these communities have left an extensive fossil record. They are fossilized in structures called stromatilites, dome-shaped mounds formed by the merger of mineral sediments into microbial mats.

Mammals and flowering plants are relative newcomers and only appeared around 100 million years ago.

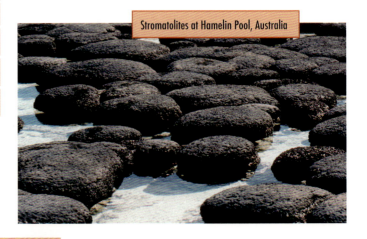
Stromatolites at Hamelin Pool, Australia

MICROBES AND THE HUMAN BODY

CHAPTER 2

MICROBES AND THE HUMAN BODY

Have you ever wondered why when we are surrounded by microbes we are not ill all the time?

Microbes and disease

A few harmful microbes, for example less than 1 % of bacteria, can invade our body (the host) and make us ill. Microbes cause infectious diseases such as 'flu and measles. There is also strong evidence that microbes may contribute to many non–infectious chronic diseases such as some forms of cancer and coronary heart disease. Different diseases are caused by different types of micro-organisms. Microbes that cause disease are called pathogens.

Infectious disease	Microbe that causes the disease	Type of microbe
Cold	Rhinovirus	Virus
Chickenpox	Varicella zoster	Virus
German measles	Rubella	Virus
Whooping cough	*Bordatella pertussis*	Bacterium
Bubonic plague	*Yersinia pestis*	Bacterium
TB (Tuberculosis)	*Mycobacterium tuberculosis*	Bacterium
Malaria	*Plasmodium falciparum*	Protozoan
Ringworm	*Trichophyton rubrum*	Fungus
Athletes' foot	*Trichophyton mentagrophytes*	Fungus

Invading microbes

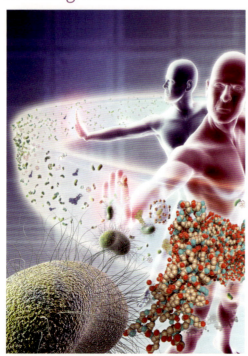

Microbes mainly get into our body through the nose, mouth, urinary system and wounds to the skin. Once inside the microbes multiply at an amazing rate. Bacteria, in optimum conditions, can divide into two every twenty minutes (see page 12) and viruses take over cells to make huge numbers of copies of themselves (see page 13). To make us ill microbes have to

reach their target site in the body

attach to the target site they are trying to infect so that they are not dislodged.

multiply rapidly

obtain their nutrients from the host

avoid and survive attack by the host's immune system (see page 17).

MICROBES AND THE HUMAN BODY

The immune system

An infection can be seen as a battle between the invading pathogens and the host. Our bodies are equipped to fight off invading microbes that may cause disease. These are called our natural defences.

Computer artwork of bacteria (blue and green) on human skin

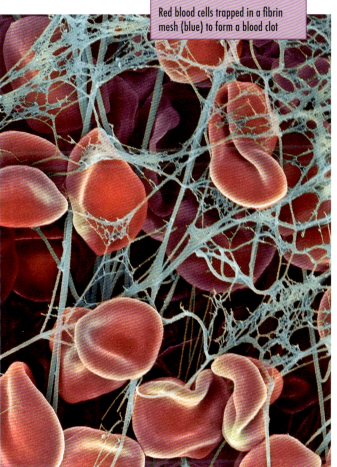

Red blood cells trapped in a fibrin mesh (blue) to form a blood clot

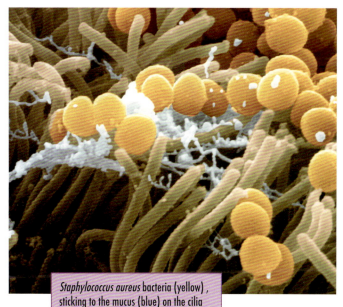

Staphylococcus aureus bacteria (yellow), sticking to the mucus (blue) on the cilia

First line of defence

The first line of defence is non-specific and aims to stop microbes from entering the body. The skin and mucous membranes act as a physical barrier preventing penetration by microbes.

If the skin is cut then the blood produces a clot which seals the wound and prevents microbes from entering. A clot is formed when the platelets found in the blood clump together at the site of the wound and release a chemical called clotting factor which attracts more platelets to the site. The platelets form a weak plug. Fibrin, a protein found in blood, forms a mesh of fibres at the site of the wound, which binds the various blood cells, including red blood cells and platelets, together forming a solid structure called a blood clot. The fibrin, which is insoluble, hardens and dries to form a tough scab.

The surfaces of the body – the skin, digestive system, and the lining of the nose – are covered by a community of microbes called the normal body flora. They help to protect a host from becoming infected with more harmful micro-organisms by also acting as a physical barrier. The normal body flora colonises these linings which reduces the area available for pathogens to attach to and become established. It also means that the harmful microbes have to compete with the normal body flora for nutrients.

MICROBES AND THE HUMAN BODY

Factlet
Healthy guts!
Most of the body's bacteria live in the large intestine. The average human gut contains around 1 kg of these good bacteria which is equivalent to one bag of sugar. Over 400 different types of bacteria live in the gut. Bifidobacteria are one of the most common and important groups of friendly bacteria found there.

Bifidobacteria along with other beneficial bacteria are now being added to foods such as yoghurt. These foods are called probiotic (for life) foods. If these microbes are able to survive the acid environment of the stomach and arrive safely in the large intestine, it is hoped that they will increase the proportion of beneficial micro-organisms present. This may be particularly useful after a person has been ill, for example with diarrhoea, or has been taking antibiotics which will have killed the normal gut flora along with the pathogen.

The respiratory system – the nose and passageways leading to the lungs – is lined with cells that produce sticky fluid called mucus that traps invading microbes and dust. Tiny hairs called cilia move in a wave-like motion and waft the microbes and dust particles up to the throat, where they are either coughed or sneezed out or swallowed and then passed out of the body in faeces.

The body produces several antimicrobial substances that kill or stop microbes from growing. For example the enzymes in tears and saliva break down bacteria.

The stomach produces acid which destroys many of the microbes that enter the body in food and drink.

Urine as it flows through the urinary system flushes microbes out of the bladder and urethra.

Second line of defence
If microbes do manage to get inside the body then the second line of defence is activated. This is also non-specific as it stops any type of microbe. Different types of white bloods cells are involved in a range of activities that inhibit or destroy pathogens once they are in the body. They are able to pass through the small blood vessels, capillaries, into the surrounding tissue to kill the invaders. White blood cells carry out a range of responses some of which are highlighted in the box opposite.

A macrophage engulfing a bacterium

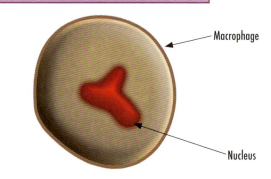

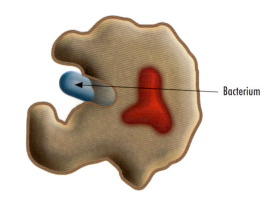

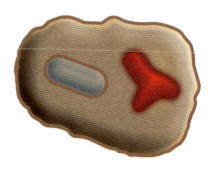

MICROBES AND THE HUMAN BODY

Activities of different white blood cells in the immune response

Phagocytes are amoeboid like cells that have flowing cytoplasm which allows them to surround the invading microbe and engulf it using pseudopodia (see page 18). The phagocyte then releases digestive enzymes which break down the trapped microbe before it can do any harm. This process is called phagocytosis. The diagram opposite shows how the phagocyte engulfs the pathogen.

Phagocytes can be divided into two separate groups:-

Neutrophils are the most common type of white blood cell and they have a short lifespan of less than a day. They destroy invading pathogens by phagocytosis. They are the first white blood cells on the scene after micro-organisms have invaded the body and are attracted to the site of infection by chemicals released by the microbe. The pus that is often seen at the site of a wound is formed by a collection of dead neutrophils and the debris they have produced.

Macrophages are the largest of all the white blood cells and they live longer than neutrophils. They engulf, by phagocytosis, any foreign material including pathogens and dead neutrophils.
Therefore macrophages are responsible for cleaning up pus, which is part of the healing process. They also release chemicals which allow the cells of the immune system to communicate with one another. Each chemical performs a specific function, for example raising body temperature (see page 21)

Basophils release a chemical called histamine which encourages inflammation (see page 21).

Eosinophils produce antimicrobial substances and they also carry out phagocytosis on the larger, non-microbial parasites, such as tapeworms and round worms.

Immune response

The third and final line of defence is the immune response. The invading microbe or pathogen is called an antigen. It is regarded as a threat by the immune system and is capable of stimulating an immune response. Antigens are usually proteins that are found on the surface of the pathogen. Antigens are unique to that pathogen. The whooping cough bacterium, for example, will have different antigens on its surface from the TB bacterium.

When an antigen enters the body, the immune system produces antibodies against it. Antibodies are always Y- shaped. It is like a battle with the army (antibody) fighting off the invader (antigen). A type of white blood cell called a lymphocyte recognizes the antigen as being foreign and produces antibodies that are specific to that antigen. Each antibody has a unique shape which locks onto the specific shape of the antigen. The antibodies destroy the antigen (pathogen) which is then engulfed and digested by macrophages.

Antibody – antigen complex

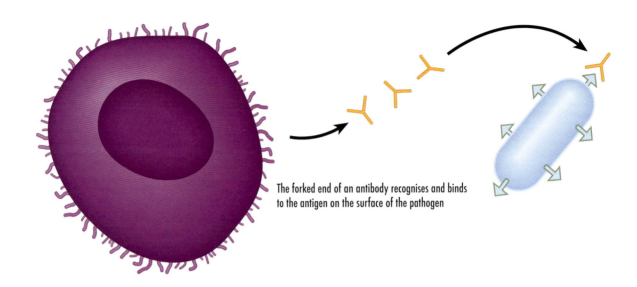

The forked end of an antibody recognises and binds to the antigen on the surface of the pathogen

White blood cells can also produce chemicals called antitoxins which destroy the toxins (poisons) some bacteria produce when they have invaded the body. Tetanus, diphtheria and scarlet fever are all diseases where the bacteria secrete toxins.

Memory cells and immunity

Normally it takes 7 – 10 days for the body to destroy the pathogen that is causing the infection and for the host to feel better. However if the human body has already been exposed to the invading microbe, the immune system will recognize it, and mount an attack very quickly – within 24 hours. The second response is much quicker than the first, often preventing symptoms of the disease from occurring which is why people don't neccessarily feel ill. This is because once the body has made a particular antibody to an antigen (pathogen) that causes a disease such as measles it remembers how to do it. When the body makes a specific antibody it also produces memory cells that are specific to that antigen. If the body is exposed to the same antigen in another infection, even if it occurs years later, the body activates the memory cells, which recognize the antigen and rapidly make the correct antibody. As a result the antibodies destroy the pathogen more quickly preventing symptoms of the disease from occurring. You are said to be immune to that disease. This explains why you only seem to get certain illness, such as measles, once.

This does not apply to all infections. For example humans usually get more than one cold or bout of influenza in their life time.

Why?

The answer is that some microbes are able to slightly alter the antigens on their surface. This means that the antibodies produced by the memory cells in response to a subsequent invasion by, for example cold virus particles, do not fit the antigen. The cold virus survives and produces the usual symptoms such as runny nose, sneezing, sore throat and headache.

Once the invading microbes have been destroyed the immune response winds down.

MICROBES AND THE HUMAN BODY

How do microbes make us feel ill?

Microbes make us ill because they either attack and destroy our cells, which leads to tissue damage. Our bodies respond to this by producing symptoms such as fever (high temperature), sweating, inflammation, sickness and diarrhoea, swollen glands, for instance tonsils, tiredness, and pus / discharge. Or they produce toxins (poisons) which can cause all types of effects ranging from muscular cramps, sickness and diarrhoea to paralysis of the nerves. Some of the symptoms are explained in detail below.

High temperature

When macrophages ingest invading pathogens they release a special substance which travels in the blood stream to the area of the brain that controls body temperature. The brain responds to this chemical by increasing body temperature from the normal 37 °C to up to 40 °C. This increase in temperature helps to destroy the invading microbe. All organisms contain protein and their cells constantly make proteins which control specific functions within the organism.
Each protein is made up of smaller units called amino acids which are joined together in long chains which then fold up to give the protein its unique shape. The sequence of amino acids and the shape of the protein determines its function in the body. For example pathogenic bacteria produce a protein which enables them to break through the host cell wall.

When the body temperature rises by 1 – 2 °C the microbial proteins start to unravel and the bonds between the amino acids break down, and the protein is said to have denatured. Denatured proteins are no longer able to carry out their functions. For example if the protein that allows a microbe to make copies of itself is destroyed, the microbe is unable to multiply and dies. It is important that the body temperature doesn't rise above 40 °C because beyond this the body's own proteins start to break down. This is very dangerous and can eventually lead to death.

To reduce body temperature, sweat is produced. Sweat is mainly made up of water which evaporates from the body and cools it down.

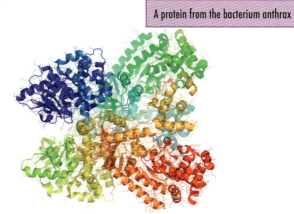

A protein from the bacterium anthrax

Inflammation

When our bodies are invaded, tissue damage occurs and the body responds by initiating an inflammatory response. This is beneficial as it destroys or contains the pathogens within a small area before starting the healing process. Inflammation is characterized by the following four symptoms: redness, swelling, heat and pain. All these symptoms may be observed in certain circumstances but none is necessarily always present. The area becomes red and warm due to an increased blood flow. This brings white bloods cells to the site of infection ready to destroy the invading microbes. Fluid from the blood, known as lymph, which contains huge numbers of phagocytes, squeezes between the cells that make up the walls of the small blood vessels called capillaries, and bathes the surrounding damaged tissue. The phagocytes immediately get to work engulfing and destroying the pathogens. The area around the wound becomes swollen due to the excess fluid.
The inflammatory process may stimulate nerve endings and cause pain.

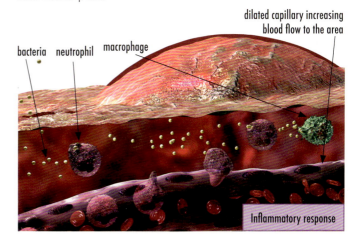

Inflammatory response

Swollen glands

The lymph removes all waste products from cells. It is returned to the blood system via the lymphatic system. This is a network of small tubes throughout the body similar to the blood system. Scattered throughout the body along the lymphatic system are nodes usually known as glands; tonsils are lymph nodes. The unfiltered lymph fluid containing microbes and other waste products passes into the bean shaped nodes where it is filtered. The microbes are trapped causing the lymph node to swell and become painful. The microbes are then destroyed by macrophages that line the surface of the node. The clean lymph fluid is carried away and returned to the blood system.

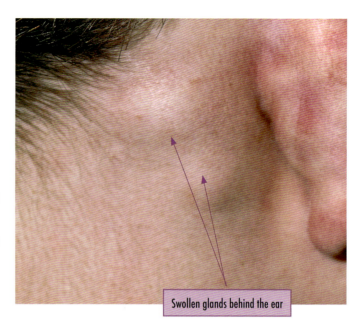

Swollen glands behind the ear

How are microbes spread?

The spreading of microbes is called transmission and there are 4 main routes.

Person-to-person

Touch
A cold can be caught by shaking the hand of a person who has a cold and who has just used their hand to wipe a dripping nose. The mucus from the nose will be teeming with virus particles such as the rhinovirus which causes one third of colds in adults. Once on the hands of the second person they are contaminated and the virus can be transferred into the nose on the fingers.

Contaminated blood or other bodily fluids
Hepatitis B and HIV can be spread through sexual intercourse or sharing used contaminated syringe needles.

Saliva
A cold or the flu can be caught from the saliva of an infected person when you kiss them.

Air
Measles, mumps and tuberculosis can be spread by coughing or sneezing. A cough or a sneeze can release millions of microbes into the air in droplets of mucus or saliva which can then infect somebody else if they breathe in the infected particles.

Food
Microbes need nutrients for growth and they like to consume the same foods as humans. They can get into our food at any point along the food chain from 'plough to plate'. Therefore great care must be taken at every stage of food production to ensure that harmful microbes are not allowed to survive and multiply. If they do they can cause the unpleasant symptoms of food poisoning such as sickness and diarrhoea, when the contaminated food is eaten (see page 40).

Microbes can be spread from one food to another during the preparation process, for example by unclean hands, or dirty kitchen utensils, and cause illness when those foods are eaten. This is known as cross-contamination (see page 40).

Water
Some diseases are caused by drinking water that is contaminated by human or animal faeces, which may contain disease-causing microbes. Clean water, hygiene and good sewerage systems prevent the spread of water-borne diseases such as typhoid and cholera.

Insects
Insects are responsible for spreading many diseases. Malaria is spread from person to person by certain species of female mosquito carrying the protozoan *Plasmodium falciparum*. The parasite enters the human

MICROBES AND THE HUMAN BODY

host when an infected mosquito takes a blood meal. Bubonic plague (Black Death) is a bacterial disease of rodents caused by *Yersinia pestis*. It can be spread to humans and other animals by infected rat fleas. People usually get plague from being bitten by a rodent flea that is carrying the plague bacterium.

Insects can also transmit pathogens to food; house flies are very good at spreading *Salmonella* and *E.coli* O157. They feed on faecal waste and transfer microbes from their feet and other body parts to food. The microbe does not invade or multiply inside the fly.

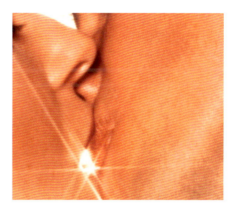

transmission of microbes

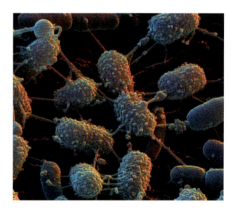

transmission of microbes

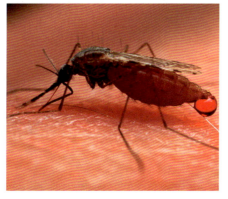

MICROBES AND THE HUMAN BODY

How can we stop the spread of diseases?

Not all infections can be avoided, but one of the easiest methods of prevention is simply by correct hand washing. In 1847 Dr Semmelweis, a Hungarian physician, was the first person to discover the importance of hand washing in reducing the spread of infection. During hand washing some areas are frequently missed and this can lead to the spread of microbes and consequently diseases. It is very important to wash and dry hands thoroughly. A staggering 1,000 times as many microbes are spread from damp hands than dry hands.

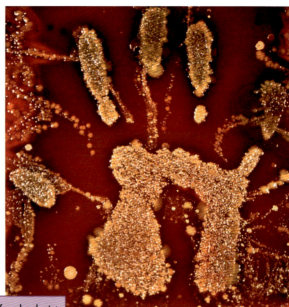

Bacteria on agar from hand print

History

Dr Semmelweis, a doctor working in maternity hospitals in Hungary, was puzzled by the high death rate of mothers from puerperal fever following childbirth, particularly in the hospital run by doctors as opposed to midwives. Semmelweis looked to see if there were any differences in practice between the two. What he discovered was that the doctors were often attending mothers straight from carrying out post mortems in the morgue. This meant that they were potentially carrying infectious material from the dead body to the mother in child birth. In 1847 he instructed all medical staff to wash their hands in chlorinated water before delivering a baby. The numbers of deaths from puerperal fever dropped dramatically from 10 % to 1 %.

When to wash your hands	
Before you	After you
prepare or eat food	go to the toilet
look after somebody who is sick	handle uncooked foods, particularly raw meat, fish and poultry
look after a baby or someone who is elderly because the very young and the very old don't have such strong immune systems for fighting disease	blow your nose, cough or sneeze especially if you have a cold
	empty/touch rubbish or waste bins
	change a nappy
	look after somebody who is sick, particularly if they have an infectious intestinal disease
	handle an animal or its waste e.g. cat litter
	have been gardening

MICROBES AND THE HUMAN BODY

Factlet
An observational study carried out in America showed that only 67 % of people actually do wash their hands after going to the toilet, even though 95 % said that they did! This means that a colossal 33 % left the loo with potentially disease-causing microbes on their hands. It is horrifying to think how far they spread!

☐ Preventing disease through vaccination

A vaccine is a substance that is introduced into the body to stimulate the body's immune response. It is given to prevent an infectious disease from developing and the person becoming ill. Vaccines are made from microbes that are dead or inactive so that they are unable to cause the disease. The antigen in the vaccine is the same as the antigen on the surface of the disease-causing microbe. The vaccine stimulates the body to produce antibodies against the antigen in the vaccine. The antibodies created will be the same as those produced if the person was exposed to the pathogen. If the vaccinated person then comes into contact with the disease, the immune system remembers the antibodies it made to the vaccine and can make them faster. The person is said to be immune to the pathogen.

Vaccines are usually given by an injection. The measles vaccine is combined with the mumps and rubella

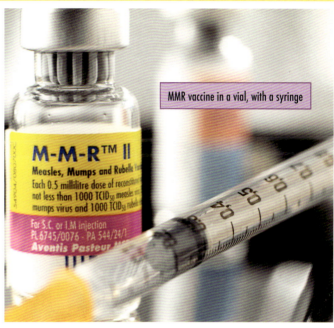

MMR vaccine in a vial, with a syringe

(German measles) vaccines and is given as a single injection at 12 – 18 months and again at 4 years. It is called the MMR vaccine. When enough people are vaccinated, against a disease, it is possible for that disease to be eliminated from the world e.g. in 1980 The World Health Organization announced that smallpox had been eradicated.

History

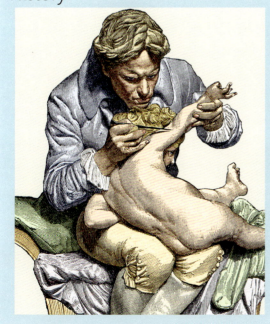

Vaccination
Doctor Edward Jenner (1749 – 1823) was a pioneer of vaccine development. During his work in a country practice he saw that dairymaids who caught cowpox from cows didn't get smallpox, the much more dangerous human form of the disease. In 1796 he took liquid from the sore of a milkmaid, called Sarah Nelmes, who had cowpox. He then scratched this liquid into the skin of the hand of a young boy called John Phipps. The boy went on to develop cowpox. After the boy had recovered, Jenner infected him with the fluid from a person suffering from smallpox. John failed to catch smallpox. This proved Jenner's theory that the cowpox had protected the boy.

Factlet
Measles

Measles (Rubeola) is a highly infectious viral illness caused by the paramyxovirus. It is usually a childhood disease although anyone who has not been immunised, through vaccination or infection with the virus, can become infected.

The virus is spread by breathing in fine droplets of liquid that have got in the air from an infected person's cough or sneeze or through direct contact with the virus. It remains active and contagious in the air or on contaminated surfaces for up to two hours.

Measles symptoms develop 9 – 11 days following infection and last up to 14 days. These include fever, headache, runny nose, cough and red sore eyes that are sensitive to light and spots. The rash usually starts on day 4 and lasts up to 10 days. The flat or brown blotches appear first on the forehead and spread downwards over the face, neck and body. Complications from measles are quite common as the virus weakens the body's immune system. These include blindness, brain damage and even death.

There is no specific treatment for measles. Patients are advised to rest in a darkened, cool room, drink plenty of fluids and take medication to reduce the fever.

Vaccination or infection with the disease leads to permanent immunity. The disease is very rare in the UK because of high levels of immunisation with the MMR vaccine. However in recent years the number of measles cases has been rising. The Health Protection Agency recorded 70 measles cases in England and Wales in 2001, 739 in 2006 and 971 in 2007. This is possibly due to a reduction in the number of children becoming vaccinated following the MMR scare when in 1998 the vaccine was linked to an increased risk in the development of autism. However, no subsequent research has ever proved a link, and the vast majority of experts believe the vaccine is extremely safe.

Worldwide, measles kills approximately 1 million children a year. The World Health Organisation has set a goal to globally eradicate measles by 2010 which will require 95 % of the population to be immunised.

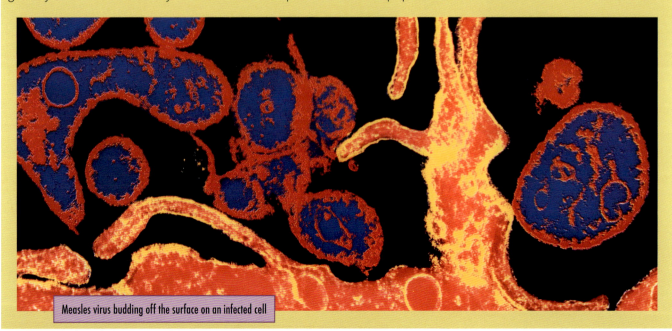

Measles virus budding off the surface on an infected cell

MICROBES AND THE HUMAN BODY

Herd immunity

Not only do vaccines protect individuals, they also provide 'herd immunity'. Herd immunity is the resistance of a group of people to an infection. It arises due to the immunity of a high proportion of the population, for example because they have been vaccinated or been exposed to the pathogen before. If this proportion is high enough then the small number of people who have no immunity will be protected because there are not enough susceptible people to allow transmission of the pathogen. The herd immunity thresholds (the percentage of population that need to be immune) are quite high. For polio it is 80 – 86 % and for diphtheria 85 %. Herd immunity will only work for diseases that are transmitted between people and not for diseases that can be caught from animals or other reservoirs of infection.

Treating disease

Antimicrobial agents are chemicals that kill or inhibit the growth of micro-organisms and are used to treat microbial infections. Many are produced naturally by microbes, but some are now manufactured and are known as synthetic or semi-synthetic.

Antibacterial drugs (antibiotics) are used to treat bacterial infections. Penicillin is an example of an antibiotic used to treat bacterial tonsillitis. Antifungals treat fungal infections, for example the drug fluconazole is used to treat yeast infections of the mouth. For most viral infections there is no specific treatment as it is difficult to develop a drug that successfully inhibits viral replication without affecting the host cell. However antivirals do exist such as Acyclovir which is used to treat cold sores caused by the herpes simplex virus.

What are antibiotics?

Antibiotics are chemicals that kill or inhibit the growth of bacteria and are used to treat bacterial infections. They are produced in nature by soil bacteria and fungi. This gives the microbe an advantage when competing for food and water and other limited resources in a particular habitat, as the antibiotic kills off their competition.

How antibiotics work

Antibiotics take advantage of the difference between the prokaryotic bacterial cell and the host's eukaryotic cell. They either

> prevent the bacterial cells from multiplying so that the bacterial population remains the same, allowing the host's defence mechanism to fight the infection.

or

> kill the bacteria, for example stopping the mechanism responsible for building their cell walls.

An antibiotic can also be classified according to the range of pathogens against which it is effective. Penicillin G will destroy only a few species of bacteria and is known as a narrow spectrum antibiotic. Tetracycline is effective against a wide range of organisms and is known as a broad spectrum antibiotic.

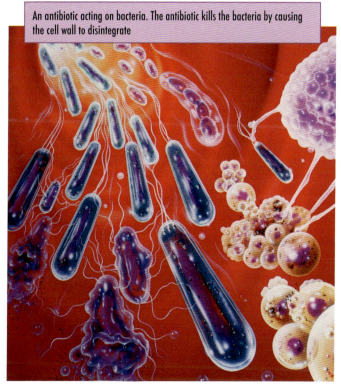

An antibiotic acting on bacteria. The antibiotic kills the bacteria by causing the cell wall to disintegrate

Antibiotic resistance

Bacteria are termed drug-resistant when they are no longer inhibited by an antibiotic to which they were previously sensitive. The emergence and spread of antibacterial-resistant bacteria has continued to grow due to both the over-use and misuse of antibiotics.

MICROBES AND THE HUMAN BODY

Treating a patient with antibiotics causes the microbes to adapt or die; this is known as 'selective pressure'. If a strain of a bacterial species acquires resistance to an antibiotic, it will survive the treatment. As the bacterial cell with acquired resistance multiplies, this resistance is passed on to its offspring. In ideal conditions some bacterial cells can divide every 20 minutes; therefore after only 8 hours in excess of 16 million bacterial cells carrying resistance to that antibiotic could exist.

History
How were antibiotics discovered?

Penicillin, the first antibiotic, was discovered by the microbiologist Alexander Fleming in 1928. He was working on the *Staphylococcus* bacterium that causes wounds to go septic. Fleming was in his laboratory growing this bacterium in Petri dishes containing a solid medium called agar. It looks like clear jelly and provides all the nutrients that a microbe needs to grow.

One day he accidentally left the lid off one of his dishes. When he next looked at it he noticed that a blue fungus was growing on the agar and that no bacteria were growing around the fungus. He saw a clearer patch in the agar.

Fleming discovered that the fungus which had contaminated the plates was called *Penicillium notatum*. It produced a special substance that stopped the bacteria from growing.

He called the substance that the fungus produced penicillin. However it took another 12 years and lots more research by other scientists including Florey and Chain before penicillin could be produced as a drug. By the end of World War II (1945) it was being manufactured in large scale fermentation tanks. The drug was then available to treat many more people with bacterial infections. Many more antibiotics have since been discovered and lots of lives saved.

Penicillin is the antibiotic and *Penicillium* is the fungus.

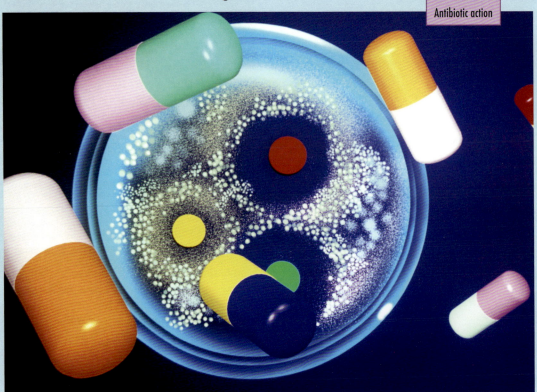

Antibiotic action

MICROBES AND THE HUMAN BODY

The human body is home to a normal flora which colonizes surfaces and reduces the availability of nutrients and space to pathogenic bacteria (see page 17). Therefore, in a healthy person it is difficult for these pathogens to gain a hold and exist in large numbers. When a person takes a broad spectrum antibiotic, e.g. ampicillin, the antibiotic does not discriminate between the pathogens and the beneficial normal bacterial flora of the body and both will be killed. A reduction in the numbers of resident flora will give any bacterial pathogen resistant to the antibiotic an increased competitive advantage. It may then multiply, predominate and cause disease.

How is resistance spread?
Antibiotic resistance can either be inherent or acquired.

Inherent resistance
Some bacteria are naturally resistant to some antibiotics due to their physiological characteristics.

Acquired resistance
This occurs when a bacterium that was originally sensitive to an antibiotic develops resistance. For example resistance genes can be transferred from one plasmid to another plasmid or chromosome, or resistance can occur due to a random spontaneous chromosomal mutation (see page 27).

MRSA is always in the news: What is it?
Staphylococcus aureus is a bacterium that is found on the skin and in the nose. It usually lives there completely harmlessly, this is called colonization. About 30 % of the population is colonized by *S. aureus*. If you cut yourself and the wound gets inflamed and produces pus, you probably have a *S. aureus* infection. *S. aureus* is the most common cause of hospital-acquired infection (HAI). *S. aureus* infects 1.6 % of all patients having operations in England. Infection with *S. aureus* in a hospitalised patient is usually minor, but can sometimes be very severe and even fatal.

Infections are prevented by good infection control practices such as hand washing and cleanliness.

In addition, patients at high risk, such as those undergoing surgery, may be screened to see if they are carriers of *S. aureus* and decolonised, or given antibiotics to prevent any potential infection.

MRSA stands for methicillin-resistant *Staphylococcus aureus*. This means that the bacterium *S. aureus* is resistant to the antibiotic methicillin – a type of penicillin. Micro-organisms are termed drug-resistant when they are no longer inhibited by an antibiotic to which they were previously sensitive.

Prevention and treatment of MRSA
Because MRSA is so widespread in our hosptials, prevention and treatment with the antibiotic flucloxacillin is not now effective. Treatment is now dependent on the last reliable antibiotic class, vancomycin. This drug does not work as well, is more expensive, has side effects and has to be administered in hospital. Even with treatment 25 % of patients that develop MRSA bacteraemia will die. This equates to approximately 2000 people each year. The UK has one of the highest rates of MRSA infection in Europe, but it is not as high as in the USA.

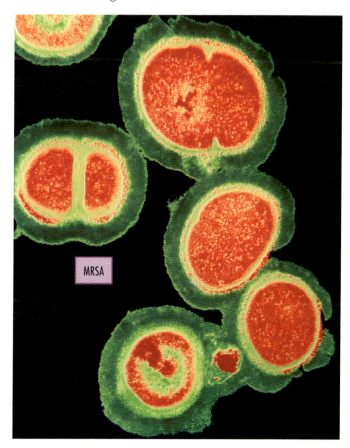

MRSA

Factlet

Sore throats and their treatment

Sore throats are extremely common. Almost every person will have had at least one sore throat in their lifetime. Most sore throats, around 90 %, are caused by viruses. The rest are usually due to bacterial infections.
The microbes that cause sore throats are spread from person to person by direct contact with droplets from the nose or mouth of someone who is infected. The droplets can be spread when we sneeze or cough, by hand contact or kissing.

Bacterial sore throat

Most bacterial sore throats are caused by *Streptococcus pyogenes*. This is usually called 'strep throat' and can lead to tonsillitis. The tonsils become red and swollen which makes swallowing painful and difficult. The tonsils may become covered by white, yellowy pus-filled spots. As well as a sore throat the bacteria cause other symptoms such as high temperature, headache and sickness.

Bacterial tonsillitis can be treated with antibiotics which destroy the bacteria or stop them growing. However they are usually reserved for treating only severe sore throats as research has show that antibiotics are no more effective at treating mild to moderate sore throats than the body's own immune system coupled with analgesics to reduce the pain.

Viral sore throat

The adenovirus is the most common cause of a viral sore throat. If the sore throat is due to a viral infection, the symptoms are very similar to a bacterial infection but usually milder. You can't use antibiotics to treat a sore throat caused by a virus because antibiotics just don't work against viruses. This is because viruses are not living cells and there is nothing for the antibiotic to work against. Treatment for viral sore throats is analgesics to reduce the pain.

Diagnosis

The doctor usually makes a diagnosis from the symptoms of the disease, but can take a swab of the secretions and send them to the microbiology laboratory to identify the cause of the infection. If this is done then antibiotics will only be prescribed if the infection is due to bacteria.

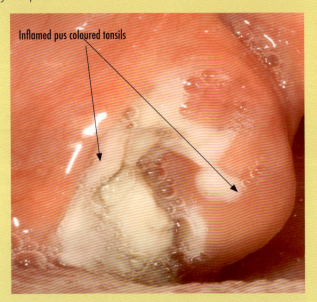

Inflamed pus coloured tonsils

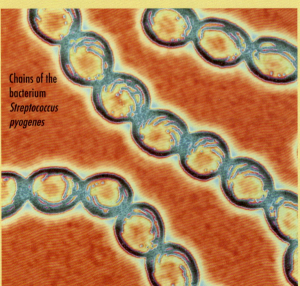

Chains of the bacterium *Streptococcus pyogenes*

MICROBES AND THE HUMAN BODY

◻ Microbes and sexually transmitted infections

Sexually transmitted infections (STIs) are caused by pathogenic microbes that are transmitted from one person to another by sexual intercourse. They can be contracted through genital contact with the penis, vagina, cervix or uterus and through oral or anal sex. Some STIs, such as HIV, can also be caught in other ways, for example through contact with contaminated blood when infected drug users share needles or from mother to baby during the birthing process. However it is important to note that the microbes that cause STIs cannot survive outside the body for long so infection from toilet seats etc is extremely unlikely.

Sexuall transmitted diseases represented by the male symbol (right) and female symbol (left)

Any individual who engages in unprotected intimate sexual contact could catch an STI - young, old, male, female, straight, gay or lesbian – STIs don't discriminate! You do not have to be promiscuous (have lots of sexual partners) to catch an STI: you could become infected after having unprotected sex just once if your partner is already infected.

STIs can cause unpleasant and sometimes life-threatening symptoms so it is important to avoid catching one. Anyone who suspects they may have contracted an STI should get it identified and treated as soon as possible. You can get screened for STIs at your local genito-urinary medicine clinic (GUM), sexual health clinic or GP surgery. As many STIs are very infectious it is essential that all sexual partners of an infected individual are traced and treated to stop the infection from spreading further.

For many STIs a person can be asymptomatic, show no symptoms of the disease but still be infectious.

To prevent the spread of STIs safe sex must always be practised. STIs require a physical barrier to stop transmission of organisms from one person to another. 'Barrier" contraceptives such as condoms are the best method of prevention.

Overview of bacterial sexually transmitted infections

Disease	Microbe	Mode of transmission
Syphilis	*Treponema pallidum*	Direct person to person contact during unprotected intimate sexual contact. Through contaminated blood products. From mother to her unborn child via the placenta.
Gonorrhoea	*Neisseria gonorrhoeae*	Direct person to person contact during unprotected intimate sexual contact. From mother to her baby during delivery. The bacteria can be picked up from the birth canal.
Chlamydia	*Chlamydia trachomatis*	Direct person to person contact during unprotected intimate sexual contact. From mother to her baby during delivery. The bacteria can be picked up from the birth canal.

Overview of viral sexually transmitted infections

Disease	Microbe	Mode of transmission
Genital human papilloma virus (HPV)	Genital human papilloma virus	Direct person to person contact during unprotected intimate sexual contact.
Genital herpes	Herpes simplex virus HSV 1 genital and oral herpes HSV 2 genital herpes	Direct person to person contact during unprotected intimate sexual contact. From mother to her baby during delivery. The virus can be picked up from the birth canal.
AIDS	Human immunodeficiency virus (HIV)	HIV can be found in blood, semen, vaginal fluids and breast milk and can be transmitted by direct person to person contact during unprotected intimate sexual contact. Through contaminated bodily fluids and from mother to her unborn child via the placenta.

MICROBES AND THE HUMAN BODY

Symptoms	Diagnosis	Treatment
Primary syphilis Painless red sores anywhere on body. Secondary syphilis 'flu like symptoms Tertiary syphilis Not contagious but leads to complications of the heart, respiratory system or central nervous system.	Diagnosis includes examination of the genitals and possibly the anus. A blood sample is taken and the sores are swabbed. Samples are sent to the laboratory for analysis.	Antibiotics can be used to treat all stages of the infection. But they can't repair the damage that has already been done to the organs during the tertiary stage.
Pain or burning sensation when urinating and a yellow or green discharge.	Cultures are taken using a swab that is wiped over parts of the body that may be infected such as the penis or cervix and sent to the laboratory for analysis.	Antibiotics can be used to treat gonorrhoea. Some strains of *N. gonorrhoeae* are developing resistance to a large number of antibiotics.
See page 34	See page 34	See page 34

Symptoms	Diagnosis	Treatment
Warts in the genital area. HPV types 16 and 18 are associated with cervical cancer.	Not routinely available but if cervical screening shows either borderline or moderate changes to the cells a women is offered a test for HPV.	The warts usually clear if left untreated but they can be removed with caustic agents or frozen with liquid nitrogen. There is no cure and warts can recur. There is a new vaccine available to protect against some types of HPV.
Initial infection is often severe. The suffer feels unwell with burning sensation when urinating. Virus becomes dormant in nerve fibres linked to an infected area. It can reactivate at any time causing blisters in the genital area.	Physical examination of the genital area. Swabs are pressed against blister, if present, to sample the fluid. This is sent away for analysis. If no blisters are present a blood sample is taken.	There is no cure for herpes and infection is usually for life. The initial infection is often treated with antiviral drugs, but recurrences, which are usually short and mild, do not require treatment.
The virus weakens the immune system by attacking white blood cells. Once HIV has damaged the immune system, a person is more at risk of developing other infections and cancers.	By a blood test which looks for viral antibodies to HIV.	There is no cure for HIV. Highly active anti-retroviral treatment (HAART) can suppress the virus and protect the immune system from damage. This prolongs life but does not prevent the virus from being passed on.

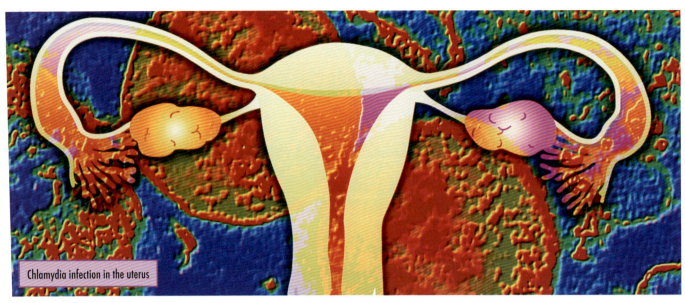
Chlamydia infection in the uterus

Chlamydia

Chlamydia is the most common bacterial STI in the UK with 10 % of people under the age of 25 infected. 50 % of infected men and 70 % of infected women experience no symptoms, but they are still infectious.

Main symptoms

Male	Female
Unusual discharge from the penis	Unusual discharge from the vagina
Pain passing urine	Pain passing urine
Burning or itching in genital area	Bleeding between periods
Possible complication: swollen and painful testicles	Lower abdominal pain

Testing for Chlamydia

Male	Female
Collecting a urine sample	Collecting a urine sample
Swabbing the inside tip of the penis	Swabbing the inside of the vagina
These samples are put into containers and sent to the laboratory for analysis.	

The treatment for Chlamydia is with antibiotics. If the disease is left untreated it can lead to pelvic inflammatory disease (PID). In men can affect sperm function and male fertility. If it is passed on to the baby during childbirth then the infection usually takes two weeks to develop and it can in some cases result in the baby developing pneumonia.

Factlet
What is Pelvic Inflammatory Disease (PID)?

PID is an infection that spreads in women from the vagina to the uterus up the fallopian tubes and then to the ovaries, causing a sudden or severe inflammation of the reproductive organs. As the infection spreads the fallopian tubes become red and swollen and the tubes eventually become blocked. If PID is left untreated the tubes can become permanently damaged which can lead to infertility.

The most common cause of PID is infection with a bacterial STI, usually Chlamydia or *N. gonorrhoeae*. PID can be treated with antibiotics but treatment must begin as soon as infection is suspected to avoid permanent damage to the fallopian tubes.

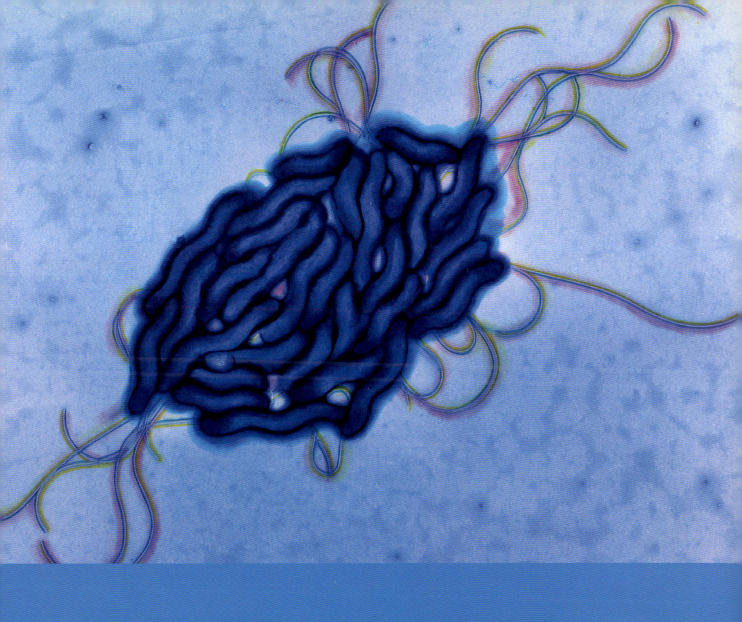

MICROBES AND FOOD

CHAPTER 3

MICROBES AND FOOD

Food for thought: this diverse range of foods – bread, chocolate, yoghurt, salami, tofu, blue cheese, soy sauce, beer, wine and ginger beer – have all been made using microbes.

Microbes and food production

Micro-organisms have been used since ancient times to make bread, cheese and wine. Food manufacturers continue to use micro-organisms today to make a wide range of food products by a process known as fermentation.

Fermentation not only gives food a good taste, texture and smell, but it causes changes that reduce the growth of unwanted food microbes. This improves the food's storage life and safety. Nowadays fermentations are used to make an amazingly wide range of food and drink.

Cocoa seeds and pods

Factlet
Chocolate

Chocolate is made from cocoa seeds which form inside pods on the cacao or chocolate tree. After harvesting, the pods are split open with a knife to reveal the pulp covered seeds. The split pods are piled in a heap and covered with banana leaves and left to ferment. The pulp gets inoculated with naturally occurring microbes from the plant, knife and workers' hands. These ferment the sugars and other products contained in the pulp. The fermentation process is complex and involves a succession of microbes, starting with yeasts, continuing with bacteria and finishing with moulds. Chocolate acquires its colour and flavour during fermentation as the chemical composition of the pulp changes. The beans are then dried and sent for processing. The first step in manufacturing is to roast the beans at 121 °C which kills off most of the microbes.

Food from fungi

Fungi have been used as sources of food and for food processing for thousands of years. In addition to eating edible fruiting bodies, such as mushrooms, directly, various fungi have been used to supplement and add flavour to foods. Yeasts are used in the fermentation of fruits to produce wines, cereals to make beer, in bread manufacture and flavouring in the form of yeast extract. Filamentous fungi are used in traditional processes for the ripening of cheeses and in the production of enzymes used in the food industry.

Bread

MICROBES AND FOOD

Fresh yeast

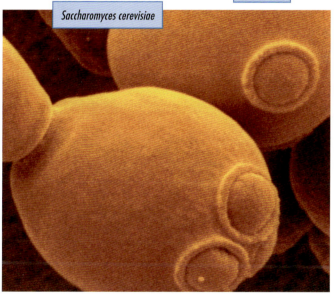
Saccharomyces cerevisiae

Dried yeast

Unrisen dough (bottom) and risen dough (top)

Bread - What makes it rise?

Yeast called *Saccharomyces cerevisiae* is responsible. Yeast is a fungus and its cells are oval in shape. Yeast, like all living things, needs food, water and warmth to grow.

Baker's yeast used to make bread comes in two forms either

> compressed fresh yeast – the yeast is alive but because it contains 70 % moisture it does not keep well and must be refrigerated and used quickly after opening.

> dried into granules – the yeast is alive but dormant due to lack of moisture as it contains only 8 % water. Dried yeast has a longer shelf life than fresh yeast and does not need to be refrigerated.

Bread is made by mixing yeast with sugar, flour and warm water. The yeast uses the sugar and the sugars present in the flour as its food. It breaks them down to provide the yeast with energy for growth. The yeast grows by budding. As it does this bubbles of the gas carbon dioxide are produced in the dough.

The bubbles make the dough expand and rise. This is because the dough is extremely sticky and it traps the bubbles, preventing them from escaping. When the dough is baked the heat kills the yeast and the dough stops expanding.

Mycoprotein

Mycoprotein has been on sale to the public as Quorn[TM] since 1985 and is a popular meat substitute, particularly with vegetarians. It is the filamentous mycelium of *Fusarium venenatum*, which was originally isolated from soil.

Manufacture of Quorn™

The mould is grown in a nutrient rich medium in a bioreactor called a chemostat. This is a continuous culture system that gives good productivity. The fermenter runs for 6 weeks and then is cleaned for 2 weeks and prepared for the next run.

The biomass and culture medium are separated and the mycoprotein heated to 64 °C for 20 – 30 minutes to break down the RNA content of the mycelium which is too high for human consumption.

The final product is collected by filtration under vacuum. A mechanical process is used to align the mycelial filaments and the resulting product is frozen for storage, flavouring and distribution as Quorn™.

Yoghurt

Yoghurt has been around for thousands of years and originated in the warm climate of Mesopotamia, the present day Middle Eastern country of Iraq, when stored goats' and sheep's milk fermented naturally in the high summer temperatures. The mixture was then hung in animal skins to cool. A soft curd called 'jugurt' was formed. This is where the word yoghurt comes from.

Yoghurt is a fermented milk product in which milk is inoculated with a starter culture containing two different types of 'lactic acid bacteria' called *Streptococcus thermophilus* and *Lactobacillus bulgaricus*. First the milk is heated to a very high temperature of 85 – 95 °C for 15 – 30 minutes. This kills off any unwanted microbes that may be present. The milk is cooled and the mixture of lactic acid bacteria is added. As the bacteria grow they use the milk sugar lactose as an energy source and produce lactic acid. The milk is kept at 38 – 44 °C for 12 hours to allow the two microbes to grow. Initially *S. thermophilus* ferments the lactose; as the level of acid accumulates it is suppressed. *L bulgaricus*, which is more acid tolerant, continues to ferment the remaining lactose. During this process the pH drops from 6.5 to around 4.5. This inhibits the growth of spoilage microbes. Consequently yoghurt keeps well in the fridge for some days. The presence of lactic acid causes the structure of the milk protein to change, giving yoghurt its special thickened texture. The lactic acid also gives the yoghurt its sharp taste. Other fermentation products such as acetaldehyde give the yoghurt its characteristic smell. Fruit and flavourings can then be added and the yoghurt packaged in the familiar pots.

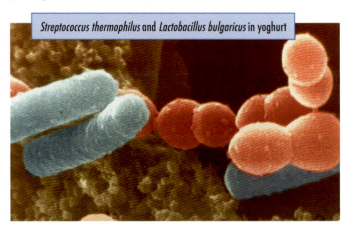

Streptococcus thermophilus and *Lactobacillus bulgaricus* in yoghurt

Food spoilage

Microbes like all living organisms need food for energy and growth. Sometimes microbes get in or on our food and start to break it down to provide them with energy and nutrients. Microbial growth causes the food to look, taste and / or smell disgusting. The food becomes unfit for humans to eat and has to be thrown away. Each food is a unique eco-system which favours the growth of particular microbes. The ways which it is stored and processed will alter this balance, leading to different kinds of spoilage.

Mouldy fruit

A mould is a type of fungus. Fungal spores (these are like the seeds of a plant) are all around us in the air. These spores can land on the fruit. If it is warm and moist the fungal spores grow. They send out very fine thread-like structures called hyphae. The moulds that grow on fruit and vegetables produce enzymes that weaken the protective outer skin allowing penetration by the hyphae. The hyphae grow down into the fruit, digest it and absorb the nutrients. These threads criss-cross each other to form a large tangled structure known as a

MICROBES AND FOOD

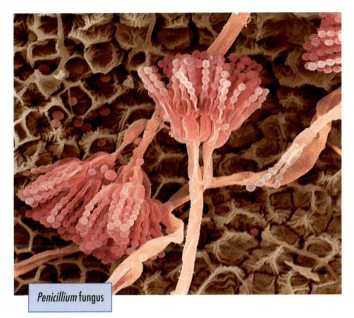
Penicillium fungus

Mouldy lemon

mycelium. The hyphae produce stalks that grow upwards. Spores form at the end of the stalks and are released into the air to start the process over again (see page 8). Eventually the fruit becomes covered in a furry coat and is not fit to eat. The spores give the mould its characteristic colour. The blue/green mould on the fruit above is *Penicillium notatum*.

Food preservation

Food preservation reduces the rate at which food decays by slowing down the growth of microbes or eliminating them. It can affect the flavour and texture of the food. Below is a table of preservation techniques.

Preservation techniques

Technique	Method
Refrigeration	Keeps food at low temperatures (5 °C or below) slows down microbial growth. Refrigerated food has a limited shelf life and must be consumed fairly quickly.
Freezing	Freezing (to -18 °C) stops microbial growth but doesn't kill the organism.
Drying	Removes moisture and prevents the growth of microbes
Pasteurisation	Liquids like milk are heated for a short time followed by rapid cooling. This process kills most but not all of the harmful and spoilage microbes present without affecting the flavour much. The storage life is extended as a result.
Heat sterilization	This process should kill all the microbes and heat resistant bacterial spores in food.
Chemicals	Preservatives may be added to food to protect it against microbial action.
Irradiation	Carefully controlled irradiation of foods can kill microbes without affecting the taste and structure of the product.

MICROBES AND FOOD

> **Factlet**
> **Spoilage**
> Spoilage is not all bad. It shows us that a food has not been made or kept in the best conditions, alerting us to the potential presence of pathogenic microbes. Also decomposition returns the chemicals in food back to the environment, to be used again in life cycles of the planet.

Food poisoning

The number of cases of food-borne illness remains high with an estimated 5.5 million people in the UK becoming infected each year, which works out as approximately 1 in 10 of the population. The symptoms are not only unpleasant, they include vomiting, diarrhoea, abdominal pain and fever; they also cost an estimated £1b a year in lost working days and medical care. Most food-borne illness is preventable. Preventing food poisoning is the responsibility of everyone in the chain from the plough to the plate. This includes farmers and growers, manufacturers, shops, caterers and consumers. The activities of food suppliers are governed by UK and EU food safety law. In the home correct hygiene, cooking and storage must be practised.

Campylobacter

The bacterium *Campylobacter* is part of the normal flora living in the intestines of healthy chickens and other animals. At the factory when a chicken is killed and gutted, the contents of its intestines, including the *Campylobacter*, could come into contact with the bird's skin. This means the raw chicken meat could be contaminated with *Campylobacter* a microbe that causes food poisoning in humans.

How do you make sure chicken is safe to eat?
Campylobacter is sensitive to heat so cooking the chicken properly will kill it and make the meat safe to eat. If the chicken is served undercooked, then the *Campylobacter* could survive and be eaten along with the chicken. After the bacteria have been swallowed they multiply inside the person's intestine and cause the illness known as food poisoning. It takes about 3 days for the symptoms of diarrhoea, stomach cramps and fever to develop. The illness lasts between 2 days and a week.

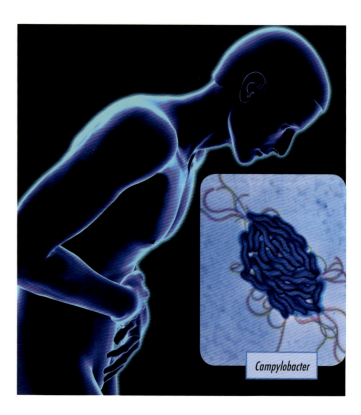

Campylobacter

Many other microbes cause different types of food poisoning. Two that are often in the news are *Salmonella* (a bacterium) and noro-viruses.

Cross-contamination, the transfer of microbes from raw foods to prepared and cooked foods, takes place by:

- raw food touching or splashing on cooked food
- raw food touching equipment or surfaces that are then used for cooked food
- people touching raw food with their hands and then handling cooked food

To prevent cross-contamination it is important to maintain good kitchen hygiene such as storing cooked and raw food separately, and good personal hygiene (see page 24).

MICROBES AND THE OUTDOORS

CHAPTER 4

The function of microbes as tiny chemical processors is to keep the life cycles of the planet turning.

The role of microbes in recycling

Microbes play a crucial role in our lives. In fact we couldn't live without them but they could live without us. That is because some fungi and also soil bacteria, called the decomposers, break down dead plants and animals and their waste products into simpler substances, called nutrients. These nutrients, including carbon dioxide, water, sodium and potassium are returned to the environment so that other living things can use them. This cyclical process by which essential elements are released and reused is known as recycling. All essential elements such as carbon and nitrogen are recycled through biochemical pathways.

Green alga

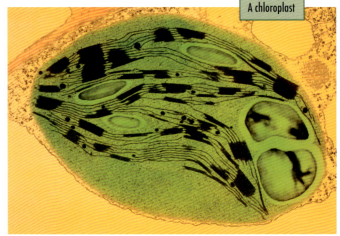

A chloroplast

Photosynthesis

Algae as well as bacteria called cyanobacteria are similar to green plants because they can all make their own food through a process called photosynthesis.

Chlorophyll, the substance that makes algae and plants green, uses the energy from sunlight. In algae and plants it is contained in a structure called the chloroplast; cyanobacteria carry out photosynthesis directly in the cytoplasm of the cell. The microbe uses this energy to change carbon dioxide gas from the air and the water around them into a sugar called glucose. The sugar is either transported to other cells and used as food or stored as insoluble starch. This process is called photosynthesis. The gas oxygen is released as a waste product. This is very important as animals including humans need oxygen to live. In fact 70 – 80 % of all the oxygen we breathe comes from algae.

Factlet
The chemical reaction for photosynthesis

$$6H_2O \quad + \quad 6CO_2 \quad \xrightarrow{\text{energy from sunlight}} \quad C_6H_{12}O_6 \quad + \quad 6O_2$$

6 molecules water + 6 molecules carbon dioxide → 1 molecule glucose + 6 molecules oxygen

Carbon, which is represented by the letter C in the equation, is being transferred from the carbon in the carbon dioxide to the carbon in the glucose. This reaction forms part of the Carbon Cycle.

MICROBES AND THE OUTDOORS

Aerobic respiration

Aerobic respiration takes place in the presence of oxygen and occurs in the opposite direction to the photosynthesis reaction. Aerobic respiration is the release of energy from glucose which takes place inside the mitochondria of living cells.

Factlet
The chemical reaction for aerobic respiration

stored energy
$$C_6H_{12}O_6 + 6O_2 \longrightarrow 6H_2O + 6CO_2 + \text{energy}$$

1 molecule glucose + 6 molecules oxygen → 6 molecules water + 6 molecules carbon dioxide

This reaction forms part of the Carbon Cycle.

The Carbon Cycle

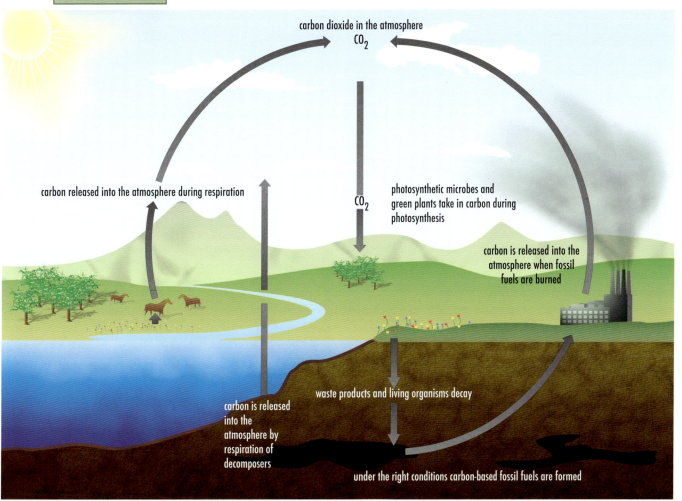

MICROBES AND THE OUTDOORS

Nitrogen and microbes

Nitrogen in the air

Nitrogen is required by all living organisms for the synthesis of proteins, nucleic acids and other nitrogen containing compounds. The Earth's atmosphere contains almost 80 % nitrogen gas. It cannot be used in this form by most living organisms until it has been fixed, that is reduced (combined with hydrogen), to ammonia. Green plants, the main producers of organic matter, use this supply of fixed nitrogen to make proteins that enter and pass through the food chain. Micro-organisms (the decomposers) break down the proteins in excretions and dead organisms, releasing ammonium ions. These two processes form part of the Nitrogen Cycle.

The Nitrogen Cycle

The Nitrogen Cycle is a series of processes that convert nitrogen gas to organic substances and back to nitrogen in nature. It is a continuous cycle that is maintained by the decomposers and nitrogen bacteria. The Nitrogen Cycle can be broken down into four types of reaction and micro-organisms play roles in all of these as the table below shows.

The role of microbes in the nitrogen cycle

Reaction	Micro-organism	Conditions	Process
Nitrogen fixation	Nitrogen fixing bacteria e.g. *Rhizobium*	aerobic/anaerobic	The first step in the synthesis of virtually all nitrogenous compounds. Nitrogen gas is fixed into forms other organisms can use.
Ammonification (decay)	Decomposers e.g. Ammonifying bacteria	aerobic/anaerobic	The decomposers - certain soil bacteria and fungi - break down proteins in dead organisms and animal wastes, releasing ammonium ions which can be converted to other nitrogen compounds.
Nitrification	Nitrifying bacteria e.g. *Nitrosomonas* & *Nitrobacter*	aerobic	Nitrification is a two-step process. Ammonia or ammonium ions are oxidized first to nitrites and then to nitrates, which is the form most useable by plants.
Denitrification	Denitrifying bacteria	anaerobic	Nitrates are reduced to nitrogen gas, returning nitrogen to the air and completing the cycle.

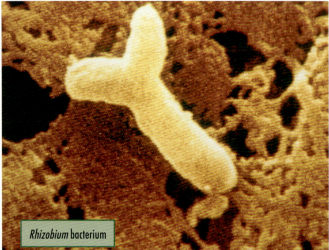

Rhizobium bacterium

Decomposer

MICROBES AND THE OUTDOORS

Nitrosospira – a nitrifying bacterium converts ammonia to nitrites

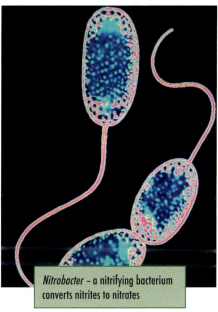

Nitrobacter – a nitrifying bacterium converts nitrites to nitrates

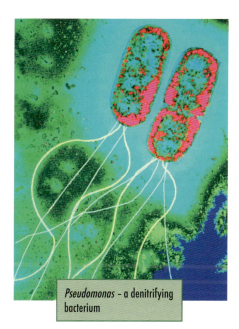

Pseudomonas – a denitrifying bacterium

The Nitrogen Cycle

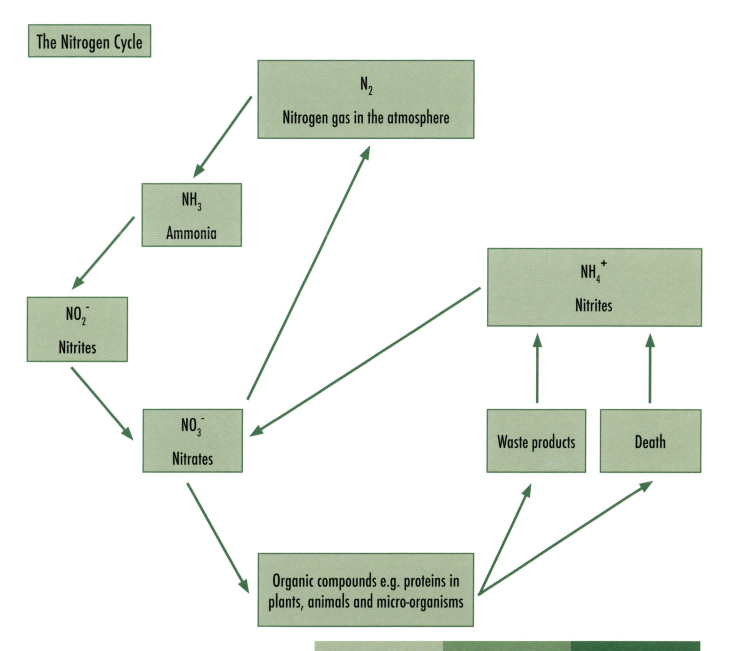

Microbes in the food chain

Green algae and cyanobacteria are found at the beginning of the food chain. They are known as primary producers because they make their own food.

The diagram below illustrates the important role that microbes i.e. algae, cyanobacteria and the decomposers, play as primary producers and in the recycling of nutrients.

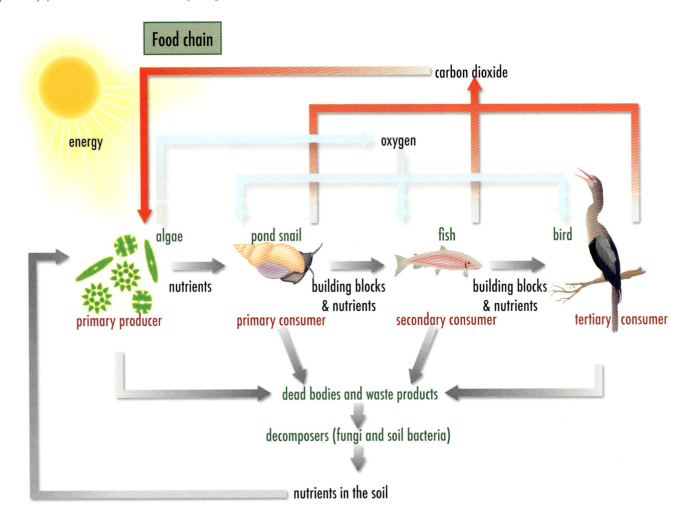

Getting rid of rubbish

The environmentally friendly way to get rid of rubbish is to compost it. Composting uses the natural processes of decay.

Kitchen waste such as vegetable peelings, fruit and tea bags, can be put on to a compost heap along with grass clippings and other garden waste. This type of waste is biodegradable, which means that it can be broken down into simpler substances by decomposing microbes and other life forms such as worms (see page 42). To the decomposers this waste is their source of energy.

The decomposition process provides the microbes with the energy they need to grow; the by-product is compost. Compost is great for the garden as adding it to the soil provides extra essential nutrients to help the plants become healthier and grow well. It also improves the structure of the soil.

Composting is very environmentally friendly as it reduces the amount of waste that is put into landfill sites. Kitchen and garden waste buried in landfill sites cannot rot properly due to the lack of oxygen. The site may start to smell and due to the anaerobic conditions that develop, a mixture of microbes break down the organic matter giving off the gases methane and carbon

MICROBES AND THE OUTDOORS

dioxide. Finished landfill sites have to be vented so these gases can escape into the atmosphere. Some landfill sites now collect this biogas and use it to generate heat or power. Methane is a greenhouse gas that can affect the Earth's atmosphere and lead to changes in the weather. This contributes to global warming (see page 54).

Landfill gas (methane) flare at a former landfill site.

Sewage treatment

Flushing the toilet, having a wash or using the dishwasher produces waste material and water. This is called sewage. It travels from the home along a series of pipes to the treatment plant where it is joined by sewage from industry, shops and offices, and waste water from roads and roofs. This effluent has to be cleaned up before the water can be safely returned to the rivers and streams.

What happens at the sewage treatment plant?

First the sewage is sieved to remove solid objects ranging from tissues and toothbrushes through to grit. The sewage, which is swarming with a wide variety of microbes, is pumped into large aeration tanks. In the aeration tanks the sediment sinks to the bottom leaving a soup on the top. Air is bubbled through the tanks causing the good bacteria to grow and digest the harmful bacteria. This makes the effluent safe to return to the river. The activated sludge is then pumped into another tank where it is heated to 350 °C and stored for 12-14 days and a different set of bacteria uses this sludge as a food source and breaks it down into simpler substances – gas, water and treated sludge. The clean water is returned to the river. The methane produced is used to run turbines that generate electricity.

Any harmful microbes living in the sludge are destroyed by the beneficial ones. Most of the sludge is dried into 'cake' and added to fields as a fertilizer.

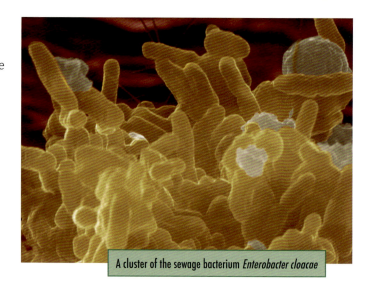

A cluster of the sewage bacterium *Enterobacter cloacae*

Factlet
Biogas
Biogas is the name given to the gas that can be collected from decaying biomass. It is a mixture of about 60 % methane, 40 % carbon dioxide and trace amounts of hydrogen sulphide and nitrogen.

Biogas generators
Biomass, which is waste organic matter such as manure, food waste or crops, is fermented in large tanks to produce biogas. To start the process, shredded plant materials and animal wastes are mixed with water in the biogas generator. The tank is then sealed so no air can get in. The biomass is fermented anaerobically by methanogenic bacteria which occur naturally in the biomass. Within days the bacteria will begin to produce biogas. The biogas forms bubbles in the mixture, rises to the surface and collects at the top of the tank. It is piped to a large balloon-like bag where it is stored until needed. The biogas which can be used to generate power is composed of 50-80 % methane, 15-45 % carbon dioxide and 5 % water vapour.

As the production of biogas slows down, the remaining waste material is removed from the generator, dried and used as a fertilizer. The process is then restarted with a new supply of biomass.

Cleaning up with microbes

There are microbes in the environment that break down toxic waste into safe matter. Scientists are using these microbes to clean up land and water polluted with oil spills, metals like mercury and lead and radioactive waste.

Bioremediation is the scientific name given to the process where microbes clean up toxic waste. Remediation means to make things right again and bio means to do it using living organisms such as bacteria.

Oil eating microbes (OEMs) use oils as their source of food. OEMs can help to clean up oil spills from ships in the sea. Oil still remains an important fossil fuel and is transported across the oceans in huge tankers. Accidents can and do happen. For example, in 2002 the ship named the Prestige began to leak large quantities of oil from one of its tanks on to the Spanish coast line. This weakened the structure of the vessel and eventually the tanker split in half releasing over 20 million gallons of oil into the sea. A slurry of OEMs was pumped into the hold.

MICROBES AND THE OUTDOORS

The microbes used the oil as their food source and digested it to give them energy. The by-products of digestion were water and gases such as carbon dioxide which were released into the surrounding water. Once the OEMs have used up their entire food source, in this case the oil, they die because there is nothing left for them to feed on.

Oil pollution on the beach after the Prestige disaster

Factlet
Alcanivorax borkumensis

One of the most effective oil eaters is the rod shaped bacterium *Alcanivorax borkumensis*. It is hardly ever found in unpolluted seas but quickly becomes the dominant type in the sea after an oil spill; it often comprises 80-90 % of the oil degrading microbial community. Scientists have sequenced the entire genome of this microbe, which uses oil as both its carbon and energy source. They are hoping to discover which of its genes are responsible for making it so successful at breaking down oil. They want to use this information to speed up the breakdown of oil spills in the future.

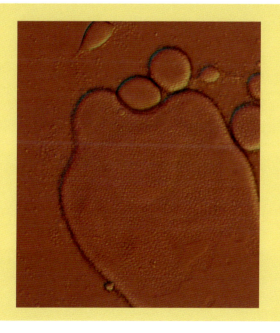

Is it a fungus? Is it an alga? No it's lichen!

Lichens are very strange life forms that are made up of not one, but two or sometimes three types of microbes: a fungus, usually an alga and / or a cyanobacterium. They live very closely together and form a successful partnership where each benefits from the other. The alga or cyanobacterium uses sunlight to make food by photosynthesis (see page 42) for itself and the fungus. The fungus surrounds the alga or cyanobacterium providing it with a safe place to live and the fungus is better able to find both nutrients and water from the soil.

Lichens can grow on just about anything found outside. They are very common on older buildings, gravestones and trees. There are over 1,700 species of lichen in Britain. They have very distinct shapes, textures and colours. They grow very slowly and live for a long time, some for thousands of years.

Why are lichens so important?

They can tell us if our air is clean. Lichens are very sensitive to air pollution especially the air's acidity. The more polluted the air, the fewer types of lichens in the area. Shrubby and leafy lichens only survive in clean air. In the most polluted areas there are none at all.

Drug companies use substances from lichens to make antibiotics.

Extracts from lichens can be used to dye wool.

There are three main categories of lichen: crustose (crusty), foliose (leafy) and fruticose (shrubby).

Crustose lichen on a gravestone

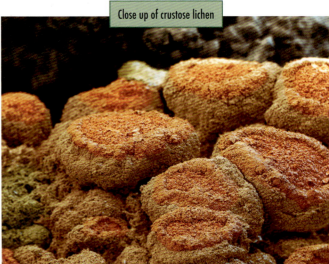
Close up of crustose lichen

Foliose lichen on a branch

Fruticose lichen

MICROBES AND CLIMATE CHANGE

CHAPTER 5

MICROBES AND CLIMATE CHANGE

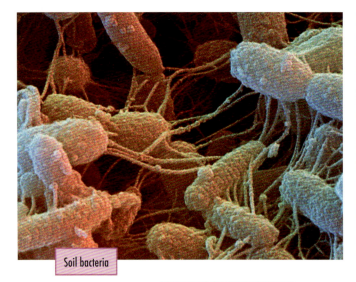
Soil bacteria

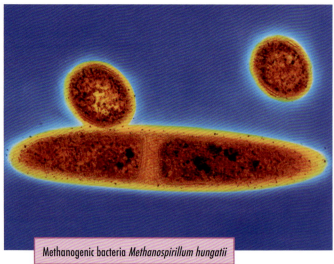
Methanogenic bacteria *Methanospirillum hungatii*

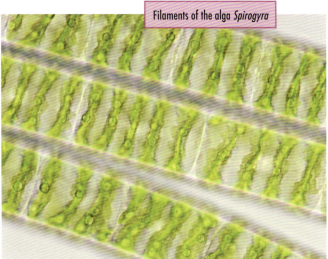
Filaments of the alga *Spirogyra*

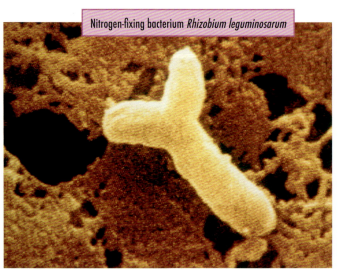
Nitrogen-fixing bacterium *Rhizobium leguminosarum*

Climate change is a hot topic – discover the role microbes play in this global challenge.

What is climate change?

Most scientists now agree that climate change is taking place. This is being demonstrated globally by the melting of the polar ice sheets and locally by the milder winters we are having, coupled with more extreme weather such as heavy rain and flooding.

The Earth is surrounded by a thick layer of gases which keeps the planet warm and allows plants, animals and microbes to live. These gases work like a blanket. Without this blanket the Earth would be 20–30 °C colder and much less suitable for life. Climate change is happening because there has been an increase in temperature across the world. This is causing the Earth to heat up, which is called global warming.

What causes global warming?

The blanket of gases that surrounds the Earth is getting much thicker. These gases are trapping more heat in the atmosphere causing the planet to warm up.

Where are the extra gases coming from?

These gases are called greenhouse gases. The three most important greenhouse gases are carbon dioxide, methane and nitrous oxide and these have increased dramatically in recent years due to human activity.

The Earth is known as a 'closed system' which means that it produces everything it needs to ensure the survival and growth of its residents. In nature there are chemical cycles such as the Carbon Cycle to control and balance these gases that surround the Earth.

MICROBES AND CLIMATE CHANGE

The Carbon Cycle is a complex series of processes through which all of the carbon atoms in existence rotate. This means that the carbon atoms in your body today have been used in many other molecules since time began, perhaps as the carbon found in carbon dioxide in the air. Microbes play an important role as either generators or users of these gases in the environment as they are able to recycle and transform the essential elements such as carbon and nitrogen that make up cells.

Bacteria and archaea are involved in the 'cycles' of all the essential elements. For example

- In the Carbon Cycle methanogens convert carbon dioxide to methane in a process called methanogenesis.

- In the Nitrogen Cycle bacteria such as *Rhizobium* fix nitrogen, which means they convert nitrogen in the atmosphere into biological nitrogen that can be used by plants to build plant proteins.

Other microbes are also involved in these cycles. For example

- Photosynthetic algae and cyanobacteria form a major component of marine plankton. They play a key role in the Carbon Cycle as they carry out photosynthesis and form the basis of food chains in the oceans.

- Fungi and soil bacteria – the decomposers – play a major role in the Carbon Cycle as they break down organic matter and release carbon dioxide back into the atmosphere.

Can microbes help save the planet?

*P*rochlorococcus and *Synechococcus* are single celled cyanobacteria. They are the smallest yet most abundant photosynthetic microbes in the ocean. They are so small that a hundred of these organisms can fit end-to-end across the width of a human hair. There are around 100 million *Prochlorococcus* cells per litre of seawater.

Researchers estimate that *Prochlorococcus* and *Synechococcus* remove about 10 billion tons of carbon from the air each year; this is about two-thirds of the total carbon fixation that occurs in the oceans. Scientists have deciphered the genomes of these two microbes.

Factlet
What is a genome?
It is a map of the complete genetic make-up of an organism. The basic units of genetic information are called genes. The genome, which is made up of genes, contains all of the biological information needed to build and maintain a living example of that organism. The number of genes an organism has depends to some extent on the complexity of the organism.

With this knowledge scientists hope to understand why these two microbes carry out photosynthesis so successfully. Ultimately being able to harness such microbial power could slow down increases in levels of carbon dioxide and other greenhouse gases and eventually reduce global climate warming.

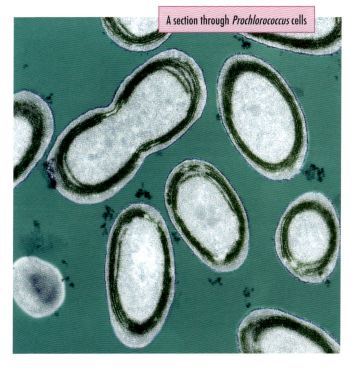

A section through *Prochlorococcus* cells

MICROBES AND CLIMATE CHANGE

How are microbes contributing to global warming?

A group of animals called ruminants such as sheep, cattle, goats, camels and water buffalo have a special four chambered stomach. The largest compartment is called the rumen. This pouch is teeming with billions of bacteria, protozoa, moulds and yeasts. These microbes digest the cellulose found in the grass, hay and grain that the animal consumes, breaking it down into simpler substances that the animal is able to absorb. Cellulose is the tough insoluble fibre that makes up the cell walls of plants; it gives the plant structure. Animals can't break down cellulose directly as they don't produce the neccessary digestive enzymes.

The methanogens, a group of archaea that live in the rumen, specialise in breaking down the animal's food into the gas methane. The ruminant then belches this gas out at both ends of its digestive system. Methane is a very powerful greenhouse gas because it traps about 20 times as much heat as the same volume of carbon dioxide. As a result it warms the planet up to 20 times more than carbon dioxide. Around 20 % of global methane production is from farm animals.

Highland cattle

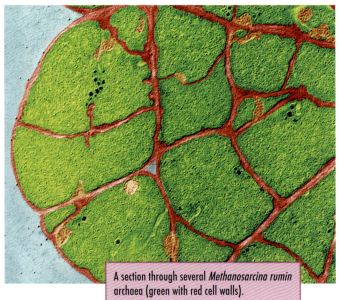

A section through several *Methanosarcina rumin* archaea (green with red cell walls).

Scientists are looking at ways to reduce the amount of methane emissions from ruminants.

One group in Australia has developed a vaccine which can be given to the animal. The vaccine works by preventing the microbes that live in the animals' rumen from producing methane. The vaccine was tested on sheep which belched 8 % less methane in a 13 hour test. At present the vaccine is only effective against 20 % of the microbial species that produce methane. To reduce methane production further scientists need to develop a vaccine that is active against more of the archaea that produce methane.

The scientists were concerned that stopping the methanogens from working might affect the digestion of the ruminants and result in the animal being smaller. However what they did find is that cutting down the amount of methane an animal produces actually boosts its growth. This is because the process of methanogenesis uses energy which can result in a small but significant loss of energy available to an animal.

Another group of researchers is investigating the use of food additives in the diet of cattle to see if it will reduce the amount of methane they emit.

MICROBES AND CLIMATE CHANGE

The role of soil microbes in climate change

Soil is not a sterile substance. It is home to a vast array of life ranging from moles to microbes. This makes it a very active substance.

As the climate heats up it is predicted that the activity of microbes responsible for the breakdown of carbon-based materials in the soil will speed up. If this happens then even more carbon dioxide will be released into the environment. This is because increased microbial activity results in an increase in respiration, which produces more carbon dioxide as a waste product.

Experiments in the laboratory have shown that soil respiration and carbon dioxide release can double with every 5-10 °C increase in temperature. A vicious cycle is set up. As more carbon dioxide is released it causes global warming, which in turn speeds up the activity of the soil microbes again. Researchers are carrying out investigations to see if this theory is correct and if microbes in their natural habitat will speed up their activity as it gets warmer and increase global warming.

Factlet
What is a carbon neutral fuel?

If biofuels, which are made from living things or the waste that they produce, can be made without using huge amounts of energy then they would be carbon neutral. This means that when they are burned the amount of carbon dioxide released into the atmosphere is similar to the amount absorbed by the growing plant when it carries out photosynthesis. At present a large amount of energy, provided by fossil fuels, is required to grow the biofuel crops, transport them and process them into ethanol. When fossil fuels are burned they release huge amounts of stored carbon that have been trapped for thousands of years: releasing the stored carbon upsets the Carbon Cycle. At present biofuels are not carbon neutral.

MICROBES AND CLIMATE CHANGE

Microbes and biofuels

Biofuels are made from living things or the waste that they produce. One of the most common biofuels, ethanol, is produced from plants. The plant material used is the edible part of the plant such as sugar cane (Brazil) and sugar beet (France) or corn kernels (USA) because it can easily be broken down to sugar (glucose). The sugar can then be fermented (broken down) to ethanol by microbes such as the yeast *Saccharomyces cerevisiae*.

Not only is it expensive to convert edible plant material into ethanol; ethical issues are also involved. It has been argued that we shouldn't grow food stuffs for fuel when people in some developing countries don't have enough to eat. There is a worry that Brazil will remove large sections of their rainforest to produce sugar cane. This is an issue because the trees in the rainforest use up huge amounts of carbon dioxide while carrying out photosynthesis. As a result biofuels from food stuffs such as sugar cane are unlikely to provide a long term solution as a replacement to fossil fuels.

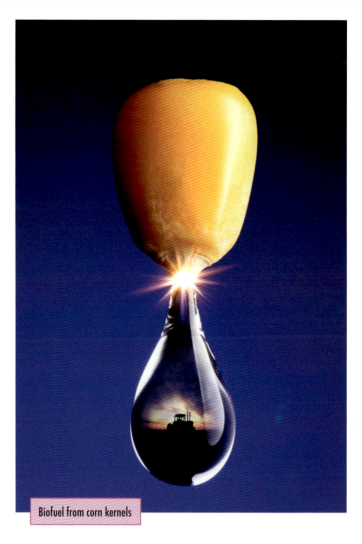
Biofuel from corn kernels

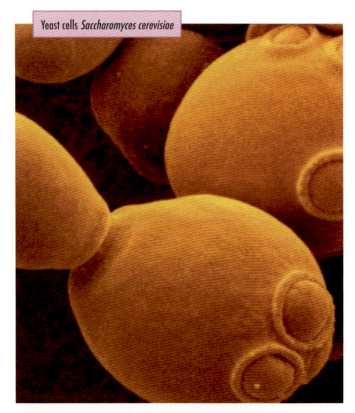
Yeast cells *Saccharomyces cerevisiae*

Ethanol biofuel factory

MICROBES AND CLIMATE CHANGE

New ways of producing biofuels

Scientists are investigating the use of cellulose to produce ethanol. The ethanol produced from cellulose is exactly the same as the ethanol that is created from edible plant parts. Cellulose ethanol is produced from lignocellulose which is a mixture of lignin, hemicellulose and cellulose. These three materials make up the plant cell wall. The lignin is the glue that holds the cellulose fibres together and gives the plant its rigidity. The lignocellulose is the part of the plant that remains undigested by humans and most animals i.e. it is a non-foodstuff e.g. stalks, sawdust and wood chip. Nearly 430 million tons of plant waste are produced from just farmland every year, not including the waste from forestry operations. There is a huge amount of non-edible plant waste to recycle.

Cellulose is made up of long chains of repeated units of glucose. Hemicellulose is made up of various monosaccharide sugars. It is extremely difficult to breakdown cellulose and convert it into sugars which can then be fermented to produce ethanol because the cellulose is tightly wrapped in lignin.

Scientists have turned to their attention to microbes to see if they can find any that are capable of converting the cellulose and even hemicellulose in lignocellulose into ethanol. The remaining lignin by-product can be burned to produce energy. They have looked in the strangest of places from termites' stomachs to the soil surrounding volcanoes. What they have found is a range of very different microbes that all have one thing in common - they produce a group of enzymes called cellulase.

Factlet
What is an enzyme?
An enzyme is a protein that starts or speeds up a chemical reaction. Every chemical reaction in living organisms is helped by an enzyme. Cellulase speeds up the breakdown of cellulose into sugars.

An archaeon *Sulfolobus solfataricus* lives in volcanic pools near Mount Vesuvius in Italy. It produces cellulase. Researchers are looking at ways of genetically modifying this microbe to see if they can get it to improve its performance and produce more cellulase. In the future *S. solfataricus* may be used to produce biofuel.

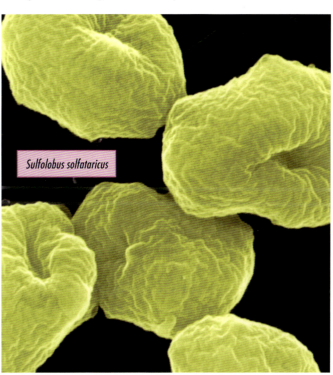
Sulfolobus solfataricus

Termites, which are insects, in nature eat woody plants like trees. When they infest human homes they eat the wood in the house such as doors and also paper products like books. This is because in the termite's stomach there are more than a hundred different species of microbe, many of which are found nowhere else on earth. Scientists are interested in a group of bacteria that digest the termite foodstuffs such as wood and grass. These bacteria produce the enzyme cellulase which breaks down cellulose into sugars. Without these bacteria the termites would die as they couldn't digest their woody diet.

Termites

MICROBES AND CLIMATE CHANGE

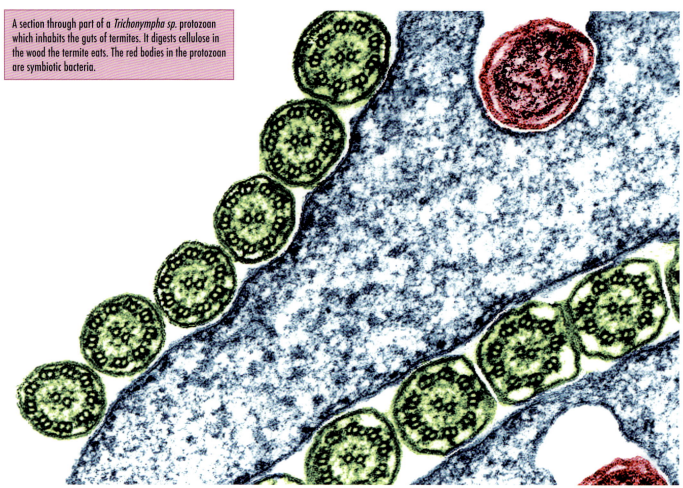

A section through part of a *Trichonympha sp.* protozoan which inhabits the guts of termites. It digests cellulose in the wood the termite eats. The red bodies in the protozoan are symbiotic bacteria.

The scientists are hoping to find the genes that control the cellulase enzymes and then put them into another bacterium that is much easier to grow in the laboratory. They are also hoping to add the microbial genes that are responsible for the breakdown of the sugar into ethanol. This genetically modified bacterium, with its new set of genes, will then, it is hoped, be able to do both steps in the production of biofuel.

Another common wood digester is the fungus *Trichoderma reesei*. It is found in nearly all soils and secretes huge quantities of cellulase. The fungus was originally discovered by the United States army during the Second World War. It was responsible for breaking down the cellulose in the soldiers' canvas tents and uniforms which meant they became very holey. It was known as 'jungle rot'.

A company in Canada has harnessed the microbes' ability to convert straw into glucose. The company genetically modified the fungus so that it produces even larger quantities of cellulase. A staggering 75 % of the straw fibre is converted into sugar. The left over woody matter, lignin, is dried and then pressed into burnable cakes. The glucose is then fermented with yeast to produce the biofuel ethanol.

Microbes could well be the key to powering cars in an environmentally sound way and in the not too distant future we could all be fuelling up at the pump with cellulose ethanol!

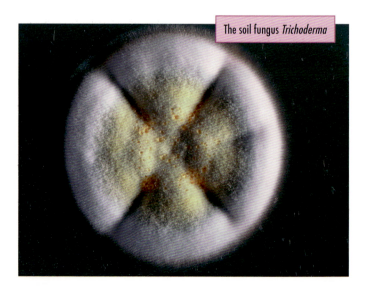

The soil fungus *Trichoderma*

MICROBES AND CLIMATE CHANGE

The impact of climate change on health

There are concerns that some of the effects of climate change will increase the global burden of disease. Changes to rainfall patterns could reduce fresh water supplies. Lack of water already affects 25 % of the world's population and is likely to get worse in some places. This will compromise hygiene and health, and lead to the increased incidence of illnesses such as trachoma (that can cause blindness) and diarrhoea. Diarrhoeal diseases already kill more than 1.8 million people annually. Higher rainfall in other areas and rising sea levels may lead to flooding which increases the risk of water-borne diseases such as cholera. The bacterium which causes cholera thrives in warmer water.

Floodwaters also provide breeding grounds for disease vectors such as mosquitoes. Mosquitoes are also sensitive to temperature change. If their habitat becomes warmer then their rate of reproduction increases, as does the number of bites and consequently blood meals they take. Warmer weather also extends their breeding season and reduces the parasite incubation rate. As a consequence, the incidence of diseases such as malaria and yellow fever could be affected. Mathematical models which look at the relationship between climatic variables and biological parameters such as biting rates for disease have shown that a 2 – 3 °C in temperature would increase the number of people affected by malaria by approximately 3 – 5 % which equates to several hundred million in the world.

Changing weather patterns also influence agriculture: increasing temperatures and more variable rainfall may reduce crop yields in areas like sub-Saharan Africa. This could lead to malnutrition which is a significant factor in complications arising from infectious disease.

It is not just humans that are affected by climate change; both plants and other animals, wild and domestic, are at risk. Bluetongue virus (BTV) which causes bluetongue disease in domestic and wild ruminants is carried by a midge and transmitted to mammals through a bite. For a long time the disease was restricted to Africa with the first outbreak outside this continent occurring in Cyprus in 1924. Since the late 1990s BTV has been spreading north. Some experts believe that global warming has caused an increase in midge populations responsible for spreading the disease. In 2007 the disease reached the UK. Experts believe that infected midges were carried to the UK from the continent on the wind. Animals with the disease experience 'flu like symptoms and swelling and haemorrhaging around the mouth and nose. The disease is acute in sheep with high mortality rates – up to 70 % of a flock of sheep can die from the virus. If the ruminant does recover milk production is badly affected with major economic consequences for the farmer. There is no successful treatment for bluetongue disease. Animals at risk can be given a vaccine to increase their immunity to the disease.

Midge biting the host

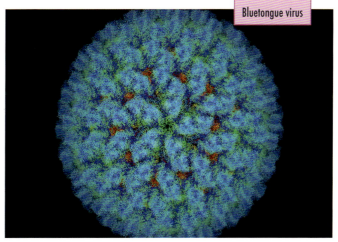
Bluetongue virus

Glossary

Aa

Aerobic respiration – the chemical process in cells and tissues, by which organisms obtain energy. Aerobic means that the respiration takes place using oxygen.

Alga (algae, plural) – a single-celled or multicellular eukaryotic, photosynthetic organism.

Amino acid – the basic building block of a protein.

Antibiotic – a chemical that kills or inhibits the growth of bacteria and is used to treat bacterial infections.

Antibody – a Y-shaped protein made by certain white blood cells which is produced by the body's immune system in response to a foreign substance (antigen). The antibody destroys the antigen.

Antigen – a foreign substance such as a pathogen that stimulates the body's immune system to produce antibodies.

Archaean (archaea, plural) – a prokaryotic, single celled organism.

Bb

Bacterium (bacteria, plural) – a prokaryotic, single celled organism.

Binary fission – a type of asexual reproduction in which the cell divides into two separate daughter cells each with identical DNA.

Biogas – a gas that is produced from the anaerobic (without oxygen) decomposition of organic matter.

Bioremediation – the use of microbes to break down toxic or unwanted substances.

Budding – a type of asexual reproduction in which an outgrowth forms from the parent cell. It then usually pinches off to form a separate independent cell.

Cc

Capsid – the protein coat surrounding a virus.

Cell – the basic unit of all living things. Chlorophyll – a green photosynthetic pigment usually found in organelles called chloroplasts.

Chromosome – a long continuous pieces of DNA that carries genetic information.

Cilium (cilia, plural) – a tiny hair-like structure on the surface of some micro-organisms or cells which beats rhythmically to either propel trapped material out of the body, for example in the lungs, or make a free-living microbe move.

Dd

Decomposer – the name given to some fungi and soil bacteria that break down dead animals and plants and their waste products into simpler substances called nutrients.

DNA – deoxyribonucleic acid: the store of genetic information inside living cells and many viruses.

Ee

Enzyme – a protein that facilitates a biochemical reaction by speeding up the rate at which it takes place within cells.

Eukaryote – a single-celled or multicellular organism which has a true membrane-bound nucleus and membrane bound organelles.

Extremophile – a microbe that positively thrives in environments that would kill other organisms.

Ff

Fermentation – the conversion of organic compounds such as carbohydrate into simpler substances by microbes, usually under anaerobic conditions (with no oxygen present). Energy is produced.

Flagellum (flagella, plural) – a long thin appendage present on the surface of some cells such as bacteria and protoctista which enables them to move.

Food poisoning – any illness caused by eating food contaminated by pathogenic microbes.

Food spoilage – changes in appearance, flavour, odour, and other qualities of the food due to microbial growth which causes it to deteriorate and spoil by decay.

Fungus (fungi, plural) – a eukaryotic, non photosynthetic, spore forming organism. They range from single celled organisms to very complex multicellular organisms.

Gg

Gene – basic unit of inheritance located on a chromosome. A gene is a piece of deoxyribonucleic acid (DNA) that contains the instructions for the production of a specific protein.

Generation time – the time taken for a population of micro-organisms to double in number.

Genome – the complete set of all the genes on all the chromosomes of an organism. It contains all the biological information needed to build and maintain a living example of that organism.

Global warming – a rise in the temperature of the Earth's atmosphere due to the increased emission of greenhouse gases which traps more heat in the atmosphere, causing the planet to warm up.

Host cell – a cell that is infected by a virus or another type of micro-organism.
Hypha (hyphae, plural) – a very fine thread that is the basic structure of filamentous fungi.

Ii

Inflammation – a reaction of tissue to irritation, injury, or infection. It is a beneficial process as it destroys or contains the pathogen within a small area enabling the healing process to begin.

Ll

Lymphatic system – lymph nodes linked by a network of small tubes spread throughout the body that transport the lymph fluid.

Lysis – the physical rupture of a cell.

Mm

Memory cell – a cell which is produced as part of a normal immune response. These cells remember a specific antigen and are responsible for the rapid immune response, production of antibodies, on exposure to subsequent infections by that particular antigen.

Methanogen – micro-organism that produces methane.

Micro-organism (microbe) – a small living thing. The group includes bacteria, archaea, protozoa, algae, fungi and viruses.

Mould – a multicellular filamentous fungus.

Mycelium – a branched network of fungal hyphae.

Nn

Normal body flora – microbes that have adapted to living on the body, are usually present and rarely cause harm.

Nucleus – the nucleus is the control centre of the cell containing chromosomes.

Oo

Organelle – a membrane enclosed structure, in cells, that has a specialised function.

Pp

Pathogen – an organism that causes disease.

Phagocyte – a white blood cell that can surround engulf (by phagocytosis) and destroy invading micro-organisms including viruses and bacteria. There are two separate groups - macrophages and neutrophils.

Photosynthesis – a process that occurs in plants, algae and some bacteria called the cyanobacteria that traps the sun's light energy and uses it to fix carbon dioxide into organic compounds.

Primary producer – green plants, algae and some bacteria called the cyanobacteria which produce their own food by a process called photosynthesis. They are found at the beginning of the food chain.

Prokaryote – an organism that has a simple cell structure without a membrane bound nucleus or organelles.

Protein a folded long – chain molecule consisting of amino acids. Each protein has a special function. Proteins are required for the structure, function, and regulation of an organism's cell/cells, tissues, and organs.

THE GOOD, THE BAD & THE UGLY – MICROBES

Protozoan (protozoa, plural) – a eukaryotic, single celled organism that usually lacks chlorophyll.

Pseudopodium (pseudopodium, plural) – a temporary extension of the cytoplasm of an amoeboid cell. It is used in both motility and feeding.

Rr

Recycling – a cyclical process by which essential elements are released into the environment where they are then reused.

Ss

Sporangium (sporagia plural) – a sac containing spores that develops from the fruiting body of a fungus.

Spore – a general term for a dormant stage in an orgainisms life cycle. Spores enable survival of adverse conditions, distribution, and reproduction. There are many types which may be produced both asexually and sexually.

Tt

Toxin – any substance that is poisonous to other organisms.

Vv

Vaccine – a special type of medicine that is given to both people and animals to artificially increase immunity to a particular disease and to prevent an infectious disease from developing.

Viral envelope – a spikey coat that covers the virus's protein coat or capsid.

Virus – an infectious particle that relies on the cellular machinery of the host cell to grow and replicate.

Yy

Yeast – a single-celled fungus.

Index

A

Adenovirus	30
Aerobic respiration	43
Algae	4 – 5, 14, 42, 46, 53
Amino acid	21
Antibiotic resistance	27 – 29
Antibiotics	6, 10, 18, 27 – 30, 50
Antibody	19 – 20
Antigen	19 – 20, 25
Archaea	4, 6 – 7, 13 – 14, 53 – 54, 57

B

Bacteria	2 – 6, 11 – 12, 16, 18, 27 – 30, 32 – 34, 38 – 40, 42, 44, 46 – 48, 53 – 54, 57
Bacterial	
cell	11
shapes	12
Bifidobacteria	18
Binary fission	12, 16, 28
Biofuel	55, 58
Biogas	48
Bioremediation	48
Blood clot	17
Bread	10, 36 – 37
Budding	10, 13, 37

C

Campylobacter	40
Carbon Cycle	42 – 43, 52 – 53, 55
Carbon dioxide	37, 42 – 43, 46 – 48, 52 – 56
Cell	2, 6, 13, 27
Chlamydia	32, 34
Chlorophyll	10, 42
Chloroplast	10, 42
Chocolate	36
Cilia	14, 17 – 18
Classification	4 – 6

Climate change	52, 55, 59
Composting	46
Cross contamination	22, 40
Cyanobacteria	14, 42, 46, 53

D

Decomposer	7, 42 – 44, 46, 53
DNA	6, 12, 13

E

Enzyme	8, 38, 54, 57 – 58
Eukaryotic	4 – 5, 14
Extremophile	7

F

Fermentation	28, 36, 38
Fibrin	17
Flagella	14
Fleming, Alexander	28
Food	
chain	46
poisoning	22, 40
preservation	38 – 39
spoilage	38 – 39
Fungi	7 – 10, 14, 36, 42, 44, 58

G

Genome	49, 53
Global warming	47, 52, 54 – 55

H

Herd immunity	27
Hyphae	8 – 10, 38 – 39

I

Inflammation	19, 21, 34
Immune	
response	19, 25
system	17 – 20

J

Jenner, Edward	25

THE GOOD, THE BAD & THE UGLY – MICROBES

L

Lichen	10, 49 – 50
Lymph	21 – 22
Lysis	13

M

Macrophage	18 – 19, 21 – 22
Measles	22, 26
Memory cells	20
Methane	13, 46, 48, 52 – 54
Methanogens	13, 53 – 54
Micro-organism	
definition	2
motility	14
range	7 – 13
size	2
Mould	8, 38 – 39, 54
MRSA	29
Mushroom	8 – 10
Mycelium	8 – 10, 38 – 39
Mycoprotein	37 – 38

N

Neutrophil	19, 21
Nitrogen Cycle	42 – 45, 53
Nucleus	5 – 6, 10

O

Oxygen	13 – 14, 42, 46

P

Pasteur, Louis	3
Pathogen	10, 16 – 21, 29, 31, 40
Pelvic inflammatory disease	34
Penicillin	27 – 29
Penicillium	8, 27 – 29, 39
Phagocyte	19, 21
Photosynthesis	10, 14, 42, 49, 53, 55 – 56
Platelets	17
Primary producer	46
Prokaryotic	4 –6, 14

Protein	17, 19, 21, 44, 53, 57
Protozoa	4 – 5, 11, 14, 22, 54, 58
Pseudopodia	14, 19

Q

Quorn™	38

R

Recycling	7, 42, 46

S

Saccharomyces cerevisiae	10, 37, 56
Semmelweis	24
Sewage	47 – 48
Spore	8 – 9, 38 – 39
Staphylococcus aureus	28 – 29
STIs	30 – 33
Streptococcus pyrogenes	30
Stromotilite	14
Sweat	21

T

Temperature	21, 38 – 39, 52, 55, 59
Tonsillitis	21 – 22, 27, 30
Transmission of disease	22, 27, 31 – 32

V

Vaccination	25 – 26
Vaccine	25 – 26, 33, 54, 59
Viruses	6, 13 – 14, 16, 30

Y

Yeast	8, 10, 27, 36 – 37, 54, 56, 58
Yoghurt	18, 38

Picture credits

Textbook

Front cover and back cover
Computer artwork of *Escherichia coli* bacteria, DAVID MACK / SPL*

Inside cover
Computer artwork of *Escherichia coli* bacteria, DAVID MACK / SPL

Page II Thumbnails
Hepatitis C virus, artwork, STAFORD, ISM / SPL
Neutrophil appendages grasping bacteria, GARY CARLSON / SPL
Campylobacter jejuni bacteria, BARRY DOWSETT / SPL
Two species of algae, DR TONY BRAIN / SPL
Greenhouse gases, RUSSELL KIGHTLEY / SPL

Page III – IV Thumbnails
Hepatitis C virus, artwork, STAFORD, ISM / SPL
Neutrophil appendages grasping bacteria, GARY CARLSON / SPL
Campylobacter jejuni bacteria, BARRY DOWSETT / SPL
Two species of algae, DR TONY BRAIN / SPL
Greenhouse gases, RUSSELL KIGHTLEY / SPL

Chapter 1
Front page, Hepatitis C virus, artwork, STAFORD, ISM / SPL
p. 2, Bacteria on a pin, ANDREW SYRED / SPL
p. 3, Gut muscle cells, STEVE GSCHMEISSNER / SPL
p. 3, Amoeba, STEVE GSCHMEISSNER / SPL
p. 4, Carl Linnaeus, SHEILA TERRY / SPL
p. 5, Hot springs at Yellowstone National Park, ROBERT ISAACS / SPL
p. 6, Cell structure, JOHN BAVOSI / SPL
p. 7, Sulphur-eating bacteria *Thiocystis*, ALFRED PASIEKA / SPL
p. 8, upper right, *Aspergillus niger*, DAVID SCHARF / SPL
p. 8, lower left, *Penicillium* MICROFIELD SCIENTIFIC LTD / SPL
p. 8, lower right, Bread mould fungus, GREGORY DIMIJIAN / SPL
p. 9, Fly agaric mushroom, SIMON FRASER / SPL
p. 10, upper right, *Saccharomyces cerevisiae*, DAVID SCHARF / SPL
p. 10, lower left, Honey Mushroom, MICHAEL P. GADOMSKI / SPL
p. 11, upper left, *Spirogyra*, BIOMEDICAL IMAGING UNIT, SOUTHAMPTON GENERAL HOSPITAL / SPL
p. 11, upper right, *Rhodymenia*, DR KEITH WHEELER / SPL
p. 11, middle right, *Paramecium*, STEVE GSCHMEISSNER / SPL
p. 13, upper right, *Sulfolobus*, EYE OF SCIENCE / SPL
p. 13, lower right, Hepatitis C virus, artwork, STAFORD, ISM / SPL
p. 14, Stromatolites, GEORGETTE DOUWMA / SPL

Chapter 2
Front page, Neutrophil appendages grasping bacteria, GARY CARLSON / SPL
p. 16, Immune system, conceptual image, MEDI-MATION / SPL
p. 17, upper left, Blood clot, STEVE GSCHMEISSNER / SPL
p. 17, upper right, Computer artwork of bacteria (blue and green) on human skin, DAVID MACK / SPL
p. 17, middle right, *Staphylococcus* bacteria in nose, JUERGEN BERGER / SPL
p. 19, Macrophage attacking bacteria, EYE OF SCIENCE / SPL
p. 21, upper right, Anthrax lethal factor protein, LAGUNA DESIGN / SPL
p. 21, lower right, Inflammatory response, RUSSELL KIGHTLEY / SPL
p. 22, Swollen glands, DR P. MARAZZI / SPL
p. 23, upper left, Close-up of running nose, BSIP, KRASSOVSKY / SPL
p. 23, upper middle, Syringe and sharps bin, SATURN STILLS / SPL
p. 23, upper right, Man and woman kissing, OSCAR BURRIEL / SPL
p. 23, middle left, Man sneezing, TIM VERNON, LTH NHS TRUST / SPL
p. 23, middle, Bacteria in frozen food, GEOFF TOMPKINSON / SPL
p. 23, middle right, Bacteria on a kitchen scrub pad, DAVID SCHARF / SPL
p. 23, lower left, Contaminated wastewater, ROBERT BROOK / SPL
p. 23, lower middle, Mosquito feeding, DR. PETE BILLINGSLEY, UNIVERSITY OF ABERDEEN / SINCLAIR STAMMERS / SPL
p. 23, lower right, Bad food hygiene, MAURO FERMARIELLO / SPL
p. 24, Bacteria on agar from hand print, SCIENCE PICTURES LTD / SPL
p. 25, upper right, MMR vaccine, TEK IMAGE / SPL
p. 25, lower left, Edward Jenner, SHEILA TERRY / SPL
p. 26, Measles viruses, NIBSC / SPL
p. 27, Antibiotic acting on bacteria, JOHN BAVOSI / SPL

p. 28, Illustration of antibiotic action in a Petri dish, BSIP ESTIOT / SPL
p. 29, MRSA, DR KARI LOUNATMAA / SPL
p. 30, lower left, Bacterial tonsillitis, DR P. MARAZZI / SPL
p. 30, lower right, *Streptococcus pyogenes*, ALFRED PASIEKA / SPL
p. 31, upper right, Conceptual image of sexually transmitted diseases, DAVID MACK / SPL
p. 31, lower middle, Condom, SCOTT CAMAZINE / SUE TRAINOR / SPL
p. 31, *Chlamydia* infection, ALFRED PASIEKA / SPL

Chapter 3
Front page, *Campylobacter jejuni* bacteria, BARRY DOWSETT / SPL
p. 36, middle left, Seeds and beans of cocoa plants, JACK FIELDS / SPL
p. 36, lower right, Bread loaves, PATRICK DUMAS / EURELIOS / SPL
p. 37, upper left, Bread yeast, MARTYN F. CHILLMAID / SPL
p. 37, upper right, Baker's yeast, MARTYN F. CHILLMAID / SPL
p. 37, middle left, *Saccharomyces cerevisiae*, DAVID SCHARF / SPL
p. 37, middle right, Unrisen and risen dough, ADAM HART-DAVIS / SPL
p. 37, Yoghurt bacteria, SCIMAT / SPL
p. 39, upper left, *Penicillium* fungus, STEVE GSCHMEISSNER / SPL
p. 39, upper right, Mouldy lemon, VERONIQUE LEPLAT / SPL
p. 39, Abdominal pain, ROGER HARRIS / SPL
p. 39, insert, *Campylobacter jejuni* bacteria, BARRY DOWSETT / SPL

Chapter 4
Front page, Two species of algae, DR TONY BRAIN / SPL
p. 42, middle left, Invasive tropical seaweed, ALEXIS ROSENFELD / SPL
p. 42, middle right, Chloroplast, BIOPHOTO ASSOCIATES / SPL
p. 44, lower left, *Rhizobium* bacterium, ANDREW SYRED / SPL
p. 44, lower right, Mushrooms, JACQUES JANGOUX / SPL
p. 45, upper left, *Nitrosospira sp.*, DR KARI LOUNATMAA / SPL
p. 45, upper middle, *Nitrobacter sp.*, ALFRED PASIEKA / SPL
p. 45, upper right, *Pseudomonas sp.*, DR LINDA STANNARD, UCT / SPL
p. 47, Landfill gas flare, ROBERT BROOK / SPL
p. 48, *Enterobacter cloacae* bacteria, EYE OF SCIENCE / SPL
p. 49, upper right, Oil spill clean-up, HERVE DONNEZAN / SPL
p. 49, middle right, Bacteria consuming crude oil, CHARLES O'REAR / CORBIS
p. 50, upper left, Crustose lichen, DR JEREMY BURGESS / SPL
p. 50, upper right, Close-up of crustose lichen , EYE OF SCIENCE / SPL
p. 50, lower left, Foliose lichen, EYE OF SCIENCE / SPL
p. 50, lower right, Fruticose lichen, BOB GIBBONS / SPL

Chapter 5
Front page, Greenhouse gases, RUSSELL KIGHTLEY / SPL
p. 52, upper left, Soil bacteria, DAVID SCHARF / SPL
p. 52, upper right, *Methanospirillum*, DR KARI LOUNATMAA / SPL
p. 52, middle left, Filaments of *Spirogyra*, ANDREW SYRED / SPL
p. 52, middle right, *Rhizobium* bacterium, ANDREW SYRED / SPL
p. 53, Photosynthetic plankton, CLAIRE TING / SPL
p. 54, middle left, Highland cows, JOHN DEVRIES / SPL
p. 54, middle right, *Methanosarcina* archaea, EYE OF SCIENCE / SPL
p. 55, Growing maize for biofuel, CHRIS KNAPTON / SPL
p. 56, upper right, Producing ethanol from maize, SCOTT SINKLIER / AGSTOCKUSA / SPL
p. 56, lower left, *Saccharomyces cerevisiae*, DAVID SCHARF / SPL
p. 56, lower right, Biofuel factory, NREL / US DEPARTMENT OF ENERGY / SPL
p. 57, upper right, *Sulfolobus*, EYE OF SCIENCE / SPL
p. 57, lower right, Termites, EYE OF SCIENCE / SPL
p. 58, upper, *Trichonympha* protozoan section, SPL
p. 58, lower right, *Trichoderma sp.*, CLAUDE NURIDSANY & MARIE PERENNOU / SPL
p. 59, lower right, Bluetongue virus, DESY / SPL
p. 59, lower left, Biting midge, SINCLAIR STAMMERS / SPL

Resources on the CD
Teachers notes and student worksheets
Computer artwork of *Escherichia coli* bacteria, DAVID MACK / SPL

Bag of diseases
Background Grand Prismatic Spring, DOUGLAS FAULKNER / SPL
Varicella-zoster viruses, EYE OF SCIENCE / SPL
Rubella virus, ALFRED PASIEKA / SPL
Rhinoviruses, cause of common cold, EYE OF SCIENCE / SPL

THE GOOD, THE BAD & THE UGLY – MICROBES

Macrophage eats TB bacteria, PROF. S.H.E. KAUFMANN & DR J.R GOLECKI/ SPL
Bordetella pertussis, CNRI / SPL
Yersinia pestis, A. DOWSETT, HEALTH PROTECTION AGENCY / SPL
Malaria-infected red blood cells, DR GOPAL MURTI / SPL
The fungus that causes athlete's foot, BIOPHOTO ASSOCIATES / SPL
Toxoplasma gondii, BSIP VEM / SPL
Staphylococcus aureus, CNRI / SPL
The influenza virus infecting a cell, DR STEVE PATTERSON / SPL
Human papilloma virus particles, DAVID MACK / SPL
Gonorrhoea bacteria, SPL
Candida albicans, DR LINDA STANNARD, UCT / SPL
Noro-viruses, CDC / SPL
Salmonella enteritidis, A.B. DOWSETT / SPL
Clostridium tetani, ALFRED PASIEKA / SPL
Neisseria meningitidis, ALFRED PASIEKA / SPL

What if ...
Blue Marble image of Earth (2005), NASA EARTH OBSERVATORY / SPL
DNA question mark, ALFRED PASIEKA / SPL
Idea, PASIEKA / SPL

Concept board
Background, Soil bacteria, DAVID SCHARF / SPL
Edward Jenner, SHEILA TERRY / SPL
Macrophage attacking bacteria, EYE OF SCIENCE / SPL
Fungal spores, EYE OF SCIENCE / SPL
Green algae colonies, DR KEITH WHEELER / SPL
Smallpox vaccine, CDC / SPL
Compost bin, GUSTOIMAGES / SPL
Yoghurt bacteria, SCIMAT / SPL
Hepatitis C virus, computer artwork, STAFORD, ISM / SPL
Bacterial tonsillitis, DR P. MARAZZI / SPL
Mouldy lemon, VERONIQUE LEPLAT / SPL
Campylobacter jejuni bacteria, BARRY DOWSETT / SPL
Chlamydia infection, ALFRED PASIEKA / SPL
Sulfolobus, EYE OF SCIENCE / SPL
Ultrastructure of a cell, FRANCIS LEROY, BIOCOSMOS / SPL
Measles viruses, NIBSC / SPL
Unrisen and risen dough, ADAM HART-DAVIS / SPL
Saccharomyces cerevisiae, DAVID SCHARF / SPL
Chains of *Streptococcus pyogenes*, ALFRED PASIEKA / SPL
Methanospirillum hungatii, DR KARI LOUNATMAA / SPL
Bacteria on agar from hand print, SCIENCE PICTURES LTD / SPL
Penicillium fungus, STEVE GSCHMEISSNER / SPL

PowerPoint presentation
Slide 2, Hepatitis C virus, artwork, STAFORD, ISM / SPL
Slide 3, Bacteria on a pin, ANDREW SYRED / SPL
Slide 5, Gut muscle cells, STEVE GSCHMEISSNER / SPL
Slide 5, *Amoeba*, STEVE GSCHMEISSNER / SPL
Slide 6, Cladogram of the tree of life, NEMO RAMJET / SPL
Slide 8, Artwork of microbes, CARLYN IVERSON / SPL
Slide 9, *Aspergillus niger*, DAVID SCHARF / SPL
Slide 9, Honey Mushroom, MICHAEL P. GADOMSKI / SPL
Slide 11, *Saccharomyces cerevisiae*, DAVID SCHARF / SPL
Slide 12, *Candida albicans*, DR LINDA STANNARD, UCT / SPL
Slide 14, *Penicillium* fungus, STEVE GSCHMEISSNER / SPL
Slide 14, Bread mould fungus, GREGORY DIMIJIAN / SPL
Slide 15, Mushroom, STEVE GSCHMEISSNER / SPL
Slide 16, Morel mushrooms, JEFF LEPORE / SPL
Slide 16, Fly agaric mushroom, SIMON FRASER / SPL
Slide 17, *Spirogyra*, BIOMEDICAL IMAGING UNIT, SOUTHAMPTON GENERAL HOSPITAL / SPL
Slide 17, Dulse seaweed, *Rhodymenia*, DR KEITH WHEELER / SPL
Slide 19, *Amoeba*, STEVE GSCHMEISSNER / SPL
Slide 19, *Paramecium*, STEVE GSCHMEISSNER / SPL
Slide 20, Malaria-infected red blood cells, DR GOPAL MURTI / SPL
Slide 23, *Sulfolobus*, EYE OF SCIENCE / SPL
Slide 24, Hepatitis C virus, artwork, STAFORD, ISM / SPL
Slide 26, Neutrophil appendages grasping pathogenic bacteria, GARY CARLSON / SPL
Slide 30, Immune system, conceptual image, MEDI-MATION / SPL

Slide 32, Influenza virus infecting a cell, DR STEVE PATTERSON / SPL
Slide 32, *Salmonella enteritidis*, A.B. DOWSETT / SPL
Slide 32, *Clostridium tetani*, ALFRED PASIEKA / SPL
Slide 32, *Escherichia coli* 0157:H7, DR KARI LOUNATMAA / SPL
Slide 35, *Staphylococcus* bacteria in nose, JUERGEN BERGER / SPL
Slide 36, Food & bacteria in the ileum, STEVE GSCHMEISSNER / SPL
Slide 37, Hair follicle, STEVE GSCHMEISSNER / SPL
Slide 38, Macrophage attacking bacteria, EYE OF SCIENCE / SPL
Slide 40, Coronavirus, RUSSELL KIGHTLEY / SPL
Slide 41, Antibody, ALFRED PASIEKA / SPL
Slide 46, Close-up of running nose, BSIP, KRASSOVSKY / SPL
Slide 46, Syringe and sharps bin, SATURN STILLS / SPL
Slide 46, Man and woman kissing, OSCAR BURRIEL / SPL
Slide 46, Man sneezing, TIM VERNON, LTH NHS TRUST / SPL
Slide 46, Bacteria in frozen food, GEOFF TOMPKINSON / SPL
Slide 46, Bacteria on a kitchen scrub pad, DAVID SCHARF / SPL
Slide 46, Contaminated wastewater, ROBERT BROOK / SPL
Slide 46, Mosquito feeding on human skin, DR. PETE BILLINGSLEY, UNIVERSITY OF ABERDEEN / SINCLAIR STAMMERS / SPL
Slide 46, Bad food hygiene, MAURO FERMARIELLO / SPL
Slide 47, Bacteria on agar from hand print, SCIENCE PICTURES LTD / SPL
Slide 48, Vaccination, AJ PHOTO / SPL
Slide 49, Apparatus for production of vaccine, HANK MORGAN / SPL
Slide 50, Disc-diffusion showing a drug effect, HANK MORGAN / SPL
Slide 51, Antibiotic acting on bacteria, JOHN BAVOSI / SPL
Slide 53, MRSA, DR KARI LOUNATMAA / SPL
Slide 54, Otitis media infection, DR P. MARAZZI / SPL
Slide 55, Yoghurt bacteria, SCIMAT / SPL
Slide 58, *Saccharomyces cerevisiae*, DAVID SCHARF / SPL
Slide 59, *Penicillium* fungus, STEVE GSCHMEISSNER / SPL
Slide 59, Mouldy lemon, VERONIQUE LEPLAT / SPL
Slide 61, *Salmonella enteritidis*, A.B. DOWSETT / SPL
Slide 61, *Escherichia coli* O157:H7, DR KARI LOUNATMAA / SPL
Slide 61, Noro-viruses, CDC / SPL
Slide 62, *Aspergillus* fungi growing on compost, EYE OF SCIENCE / SPL
Slide 68, *Rhizobium* bacterium, ANDREW SYRED / SPL
Slide 69, Mushrooms on decaying wood, JACQUES JANGOUX / SPL
Slide 70, *Nitrosospira sp.*, DR KARI LOUNATMAA / SPL
Slide 70, *Nitrobacter sp.*, ALFRED PASIEKA / SPL
Slide 71, *Pseudomonas sp.*, DR LINDA STANNARD, UCT / SPL
Slide 73, Greenhouse gases, RUSSELL KIGHTLEY / SPL
Slide 74, Global warming, conceptual artwork, PASIEKA / SPL
Slide 75, Photosynthetic plankton, CLAIRE TING / SPL
Slide 76, *Methanosarcina* archaea, EYE OF SCIENCE / SPL
Slide 77, *Saccharomyces cerevisiae*, DAVID SCHARF / SPL
Slide 79, *Trichoderma sp.*, CLAUDE NURIDSANY & MARIE PERENNOU / SPL

*SPL, Science Photo Library

Illustrations by Jamie Symonds, Medium Rare
Text book
p. 2, Microbial sizes
p. 9, Mould showing hyphae and spores
p. 11, Bacterial shapes
p. 12, Bacterial cell
p. 12, Binary fission
p. 18, Phagocyte engulfing a microbe
p. 20, Antibody locking onto an antigen
p. 43, Carbon Cycle
p. 46, Food web

PowerPoint presentation
Slide 4, Microbial sizes
Slide 13, Mould showing hyphae and spores
Slide 21, Bacterial shapes
Slide 22, Binary fission
Slide 25, Viral replication
Slide 39, Antibody locking onto an antigen
Slide 66, Carbon Cycle

Licence Agreement

The Good, The Bad & The Ugly – Microbes
Text book and CD-ROM

This is a legally binding agreement between you (the school) and the Society for General Microbiology, Marlborough House, Basingstoke Road, Spencers Wood, Reading RG7 1AG, UK (SGM).

By retaining and using *The Good, The Bad & The Ugly – Microbes* Text book and CD-ROM, you are agreeing to be bound by the terms and conditions of this licence. If you do not agree to the terms and conditions of this licence, you must cease to use *The Good, The Bad & The Ugly – Microbes* Text book and CD-ROM, and return them to SGM. A full refund of any payment will be given.

SGM owns the copyright of *The Good, The Bad & The Ugly – Microbes* Text book and CD-ROM. The copyright of a number of illustrations is owned by the Science Photo Library and Corbis Images UK, and SGM has licensed their use in this work. You are not permitted to copy them or use them except in the context of the permitted use of the work set out in this licence.

You can install the contents of the CD-ROM on your personal computer as a single individual user. You can make one copy for back-up purposes. You must not distribute further copies of *The Good, The Bad & The Ugly – Microbes* Text book and CD-ROM or any part thereof, or incorporate any part of the work in any derivative product, whether sold or otherwise distributed. You can display the contents of the CD-ROM on a whiteboard , television monitor or through a projector onto a screen for your personal class teaching activities.

You must not install the contents of the CD-ROM on the school's intranet or website.

You may modify the PowerPoint® presentation for your own teaching, but must not distribute the modified version.

You may photocopy the following student activities *Helping the environment – should we do our bit?*, *Use and misuse of antibiotics*, *Vaccination just a shot in the arm*, *Where would we be without microbes*, *MRSA*, *A bag of diseases*, *Key words*, and supporting materials on the CD-ROM for use in your personal teaching activities, but must not distribute them further.

You must not lend, rent, hire or sell *The Good, The Bad & The Ugly – Microbes* Text book and CD-ROM.

You must not use *The Good, The Bad & The Ugly – Microbes* Text book and CD-ROM in any way not specified above without the written prior consent of SGM.

SGM grants you a non-exclusive, non-transferable licence to use *The Good, The Bad & The Ugly – Microbes* Text book and CD-ROM subject to these terms and conditions.

Limited warranty

SGM warrants that the CD-ROM on which the material is supplied is free from defects in material and workmanship in normal use for 90 days from the date of receipt by you. This warranty is not transferable.

SGM shall not be liable for any loss or damage resulting from installation of the contents of the CD-ROM, or for any loss or damage suffered as a result use of *The Good, The Bad & The Ugly – Microbes* Text book and CD-ROM or from errors in the content, whether such loss or damage is caused by negligence or otherwise.

The entire liability of SGM and your only remedy shall be limited to replacement free of charge of your copy of *The Good, The Bad & The Ugly – Microbes* Text book and CD-ROM.

To the extent that the law permits, SGM disclaims all other warranties, whether express or implied, including by way of example and not limitation, warranties of merchantability and fitness for a particular purpose in respect of *The Good, The Bad & The Ugly – Microbes* Text book and CD-ROM.

This licence will be governed and construed in accordance with English law.